SILK ROAD TAKEDOWN

By Curtis Green

Copyright © 2018 by Curtis Green
All rights reserved. This book or any portion thereof may not be reproduced or used in any manner whatsoever without the express written permission of the publisher except for the use of brief quotations in a book review.

First Edition, 2018

Published by David Farland Entertainment
St. George, Utah

Written by Curtis Green
Edited by David Farland

The author has written as accurately as possible from his own memories and available records. Some events have been compressed and some dialogue recreated for completeness.

TABLE OF CONTENTS

1: Baptized into the DEA 1
2: My Life Up to Silk Road 5
3: Daring the Silk Road 20
4: Into the Dark Web 30
5: The Real Dread Pirate Roberts 51
6: My Typical Workday as a Mobster 71
7: The Surprise Delivery 90
8: Framed by Nob 99
9: Busted Doors, Busted Lungs 117
10: On Becoming a Fish 133
11: Courts in Cyberspace 153
12: The Shattered House 168
13: Getting Squeezed 188
14: More Frames than an Art Gallery 201
15: The Beating 217
16: A Rough Baptism into the DEA (Reprise) 228
17: The Drug Lords Line up to Kill Me 242
18: The Proof of My Death is Highly Exaggerated 251
19: Observations from the Grave 260
20: Seasons in the Dark 279
21: Regretting My Deal with the Devil 287
22: Waiting for Justice 300
23: The Sinking of the Dread Pirate Roberts 308
24: Cops on the Run 317
25: Getting My Day in Court 353

1: Baptized into the DEA

Marriott City Center, Salt Lake City, Utah

Saturday, January 26, 2013

When I took a job working for a company called "Silk Road" on the dark web, I never realized just what a bad idea it was. You see, greed corrupts people. It got to me, it got to my boss, the Dread Pirate Roberts, and it even took out some of the DEA and Secret Service agents who hunted us down. Greed is a slow-burning flame, and anonymity is an accelerant that can make it explode into an inferno.

When the large hand gripped the back of my head and shoved it underwater for the fifth time, the first thought to cross my mind was, "How in the hell did I get into a mess like this?"

Forced to my knees beside a bathtub full of cold water, with two burly men gripping my arms, I felt my heart thumping against my ribs as the seconds stretched on. You never realize how long a second really is until you're staring wide-eyed at the cream-colored bottom of a hotel bathtub, fighting the urge to gasp and knowing there's already water in your lungs.

I had finally quit bleeding internally from my "arrest" just a week before, where the DEA agent who was holding me underwater had stomped my back hard enough to burst capillaries in my lungs. But I still wasn't well.

In their restraint I couldn't even flap my hands, the agreed-upon signal to let me up for air. I knew my tormentors only by the names they'd given me and the badges they'd flashed: DEA, Secret Service, Homeland Security, and a postal inspector from Baltimore.

With my pulse pounding more rapidly in my ears, my next and more persistent thought was, "This was just supposed to be staged, a setup. Are they really going to kill me?" For all I knew, the credentials they had waved in my face were fakes. Might they really be a hit squad sent by Dread Pirate Roberts?

No, not the black-masked hero from *The Princess Bride*—the Dread Pirate Roberts, or DPR, for whom I'd worked, had taken the name of the movie character as part of his persona. A clandestine and seemingly schizophrenic figure with strong libertarian views, DPR was the owner and system administrator of a dark-net market known as Silk Road.

I felt as if my lungs would rupture, and all my muscles tensed and bunched for a last desperate effort to flail free, when a rough hand seized my hair and yanked me upright.

"Get a picture of him looking scared," one of them said. I had no idea who. My ears were too full of water.

"Yeah, gotta make it look real," another agreed.

I didn't have to fake being scared. I was too busy coughing and choking and gulping for breath to appear anything else. Only vaguely did I feel the water streaming off my face and down my neck to soak my undershirt.

My torturers scrutinized the images captured in their cellphones, pursing their mouths and scrunching their eyebrows.

"I dunno," said the DEA guy. "Let's go for one more."

All three stared down at me, still gasping and kneeling on the Marriott's buffed tile floor in an expanding puddle of chilly water. Once more I thought, *Are they trying to kill me?*

I realized even then that they were heartless. Little did I suspect that they had already taken steps that would lead to an order for my execution.

2: My Life Up to Silk Road

This a story about attitudes we share about good and evil, justice and criminality, but mostly about me. Each of us must take ownership of our own past.

I'm not the kind of person that you would normally think of as a criminal. I've been a Mormon all my life, and even served as a successful missionary. I came from a good family. I'm also a grandpa who suffers from some disabilities.

So here is a little history. I came into the world in January of 1966 in Ogden, Utah but didn't live there long. Soon after my birth my parents moved to California, where my dad began his teaching career. We made another move when I was three, this time to Indiana, where my dad completed his doctorate degree in instructional development.

During that time my siblings began to join the family. Through the years that followed I gained eight brothers and sisters.

My parents had a unique way of showing their love for us. They didn't talk about love, they just showed it. I don't remember my father ever saying he loved me, and I don't recall my mother ever saying it to me until she lay on her deathbed. Yet I never doubted that they loved us.

I was never very close to any of my siblings. Some were still in elementary and middle school when I left home to be a Mormon missionary; I'm eighteen years older than my youngest brother. I suppose the differences in our ages had something to do with it, but after our mother passed away from cancer, my siblings grew more distant from me.

Large family or not, we never went without the necessities of life. Sometimes I felt that our father showed his love by giving us things. I'm sure he didn't think that, but that's how it appeared to me.

Maybe that's why I didn't have much of a relationship with my dad. It wasn't a difficult or negative relationship. He took us to sports events and whatnot, but when I made the football team at Dixie College, he actually seemed aggravated about coming to the games. I quit the team soon after.

We didn't have the kind of father-son bond in which I felt comfortable enough to confide in him about matters in my life. In fact, I rarely confided anything to him, ever, until after the whole Silk Road thing happened. But I'm getting ahead of myself.

However, I had a great relationship with my maternal grandfather, who became one of the most influential people in my life. My aunts and uncles told me early on that I was always his favorite.

He was a wonderful example to me, and probably the most perfect person I've ever met. He and my grandmother lived in Preston, Idaho most of their lives, and I chose to spend many summers at their home rather than going on family vacations. Those summers are still some of the best memories of my life.

I went to Orem (Utah) High School, where I was a member of Future Business Leaders of America.

I also participated on the school newspaper staff as a photographer, which led to me getting involved with video production. This was when video cameras were only starting to become popular and were still fairly difficult to operate. I became the video nerd who taped almost every event for the school.

I struggled with math through school. I just could never understand it. Though my father had a master's degree in math, he never had the time or patience to teach me. My mother helped us with our homework, but by the time we reached high school most of the math was over her head. I ended up failing most of my math classes, and because of that I had a tough time in college. That's the main reason I never completed my bachelor's degree. But years later when I got into cryptocurrency, I was able to learn the math on my own.

In spite of it all, I graduated from Orem High School in 1984 and went up the road to what was then called Utah Technical College for one quarter before leaving in 1986 to serve a mission for the Church of Jesus Christ of Latter-day Saints, known by many people as Mormons. The nickname comes from our belief that *The Book of Mormon, Another Testament of Jesus Christ* is scripture. The Book of Mormon is compiled from the writings of people who immigrated to the New World several centuries before Jesus Christ's ministry on Earth.

Young men of the Church, and sometimes young women and retired married couples, set aside up to two years of their lives to share the message. We receive no monetary pay for this, and in fact, pay our own way.

I received my mission call to the Seville, Spain Mission and served in several cities along the Spanish coast, including Malaga, Cadiz, and Seville itself.

I had some powerful experiences during those two years, though it began as a real struggle for me. During my weeks in the Missionary Training Center (MTC), where missionaries learn teaching skills along with the languages and customs of the countries in which they'll serve, I simply couldn't understand Spanish. I struggled to learn that language. For the first six months after my arrival in Spain, my mission president made sure I had a Spanish-speaking companion to work beside me.

That worked. By the end of my mission most Spaniards thought I was a native speaker rather than an American. And near the end of my mission I was assigned to be the translator for leaders of the Church who came to visit Spain, because I was considered the most fluent in both Spanish and English. I thought it a great privilege to serve in that way.

I became one of the most successful Elders in that mission and saw more than 50 of the people I taught enter the waters of baptism at a time when one or two converts for each missionary was typical.

Once I was assigned to a small town called Motril, which was close to the coast. My companion at that time didn't speak a word of English, but by then I had gained a great grasp of the Spanish language. For some reason I don't remember, we got into an argument. We yelled and screamed at each other for an hour or so as we walked along, even throwing our scriptures at each other. Both of us were really angry.

Finally, I gathered my scriptures from the ground and knocked on a door. A man answered, and he stared at us. We must have looked terrible. We hadn't gotten to the point of fist-fighting but we probably appeared as if we had been. Still, the man let us in, and we calmed down and taught his entire family. They were all baptized a short time later.

Another time, while I was with an American companion in Malaga, we knocked on a door and a lady answered. Her first words to us were "We were waiting for you." Two weeks later her whole family was baptized.

On finishing my mission in 1986, I returned to my studies at Utah Valley University, where I met Tonya, an eighteen-year-old freshman from Duchesne, Utah, where her parents ran a furniture store.

I actually noticed Tonya's roommate first, but Tonya kept coming up with excuses to be around me.

"He's really good-looking, very handsome," she told her friends. "More important, he's a kind, giving person, really smart, and a very hard worker."

She started doing things like bringing me cookies. It worked.

Eventually I asked her out. About a month after that we became engaged and three months later, on March 17, 1989, we were married in the Logan, Utah LDS temple.

I started at Brigham Young University after our marriage, with a major in psychology. I did really well that first semester. However, after our first daughter Amanda was born, I dropped out. I returned to UVU, where I earned an A.S. degree in Science and completed my minor in Spanish.

While I worked on that, Tonya finished her degree to become a paralegal. She never took a job in that field. Instead, she decided to be a stay-at-home mom, though she worked as a cashier at a local Albertson's grocery store until Amanda was born in 1990.

In 1990 or 1991 I started a wedding video company. The business plan I created and presented to the bank president resulted in a loan of about $8000. Though not a large amount, it was enough to get us going.

Our company was one of the first of its kind, though professional videographers are common at weddings now. Living practically in the shadow of BYU, the mecca for young Latter-day Saints seeking marriage companions, I knew there would be a strong demand for our services. Tonya was all in with it, fully involved, and it brought in a lot of money. I paid the loan back in full within two years.

As the video business became more successful, my father purchased some professional and more expensive equipment for us, which he also used for his own projects. We did very well for the next few years.

During that time I developed chronic kidney stones. Once when my father, my brother Darren, and I were making a video for FEMA in Virginia, I had a major kidney stone attack that left me writhing on the floor with pain. Darren, who's a year and a half younger than me and the sibling to whom I'm closest, went to a pharmacy to ask about pain medication and what he could do to help. The pharmacist advised getting me to the ER. I decided I'd be better off going home, so I got the earliest flight back that I could and spent the next six hours doubled over in pain, until I got to the ER in Provo.

By 1992, Tonya and I decided we wanted a home of our own. With the arrival of Tiffany, our second daughter, we needed a larger house, and we had saved enough to make the down payment.

We still live in that house in Spanish Fork, Utah, a few miles from where I grew up. Except for the two years I spent in Spain for my mission, I've lived in Utah since the age of five.

So, I think that you can see that I came from a pretty clean background, but then we began to face some real adversity, a string of bad luck that lasted for years.

The next year, 1993, my partner in the video production company walked out on me. He took several of my big clients with him to start his own video business. He'd never once given any indication of his intentions to part company, and I felt betrayed for months.

With the end of our video business, Tonya and I both worked at the Utah Training School, where children and adults with severe mental handicaps were placed. In fact, I worked there two different times during the early 1990s.

Tonya and I were called Developmentalists. I worked with high-functioning adults while Tonya worked with those who needed a lot more personal care, right down to changing their diapers. Most of her *clients*, as we were to call them, were confined to wheelchairs, but she enjoyed caring for them.

Mine, on the other hand, got to do a lot of things like fieldtrips. We took them to Lagoon, an amusement park north of Salt Lake City, Utah, and rafting on the Green River. For me, it was a very easy job that paid quite well and included a lot of overtime.

While working there, an incident took place that still disturbs me twenty-five years later. A co-worker became upset with one of the clients, took him in a bedroom, turned off the lights, and began to viciously beat him. I discovered what was going on, stepped in to stop it, and reported the other worker, who was dismissed at once. I had developed such compassion for the mentally challenged people I worked with that the event broke my heart.

One unit at the school was surrounded by high fences topped with barbed wire, to hold adults with special needs who had committed serious crimes, including rape and murder. One of these individuals once broke my jaw when I had to subdue him. If you ever met any of these individuals on the street, you would've never guessed they were handicapped. This made them truly the most dangerous of the dangerous.

During the early 1990s I earned my EMT certificate and volunteered on the Spanish Fork Ambulance. However, constantly seeing so many deaths and injuries really got to me. I loved helping people, but the forty-five cents an hour they paid me for gas as a volunteer wasn't worth the horrors I had to deal with on a daily basis. Things like carrying a dead infant to the ambulance often tormented me for weeks.

I'll never forget the time I saw a highway patrolman crying like a baby. I spotted him kneeling a little way off. When I approach, I discovered he was leaning over two small children who had been thrown from a car. He was totally distraught, and I couldn't keep from crying myself.

There were plenty of other horrors, though—deaths by overdose or suicides. I kept at it for several years, but eventually the scenes became too haunting, and I quit.

Sometime in the mid to late 1990s we purchased a small flower shop. I've always tried to help my siblings out, so I hired one of my sisters to work in the shop. We owned it for about six months, did very well, and then sold it for double what we had paid for it.

In 1998, my problems with kidney stones led to severe complications, and one of my kidneys had to be removed. A year later, I began suffering from an enlarged heart and had to go on oxygen 24/7. I felt older than I was.

I began trying to take-off weight and exercise, and after another year and fifty pounds gone, I was able to put away the oxygen tank.

But in 1999, I suffered a severe injury. My wife was in the bathroom going through the medicine cabinet when she suddenly fainted. I quickly caught her but in doing so, ruptured four disks in my lower back and was forced to go on disability.

In 2004 I started my own transportation company called Anytime Airport Shuttle. With my bad back, I was mostly the manager and often had to hire help to drive. I was able to keep it afloat for a couple of years until, with the price of fuel and maintenance, it began to cost more than it was bringing in. So we sold off all the cars.

Tonya has worked through our whole marriage in one way or another, from flower arranging to being a cashier. My daughter Amanda is now the mother of four boys, and our second daughter, Tiffany, has one boy, Preston, whom we are raising, due to her physical problems. Tonya sometimes says "I thought we were done raising kids," but I feel lucky to have Preston in our lives. I had always wanted a boy. He just came really late.

My wife and I were still active members of the Mormon Church. We had worked as Sunday School teachers and helped out in the nursery, but by 2011, neither of us had a job, a "calling" in the church.

I felt grateful for the good things we had, but there was plenty wrong, too, and our life was about to take a turn for the worst.

3: Daring the Silk Road

Spanish Fork, Utah

In ancient times, traders established a caravan route that spanned the world, from China to Egypt, from Persia to India. It was used first by silk merchants, but caravans also fenced stolen goods, spices, and drugs. The routes became infested with criminals, and the traders bore more than trade goods, they also transmitted their own cultures, along with diseases. It took a lot of courage for a trader to dare the Silk Road—or great desperation.

Perhaps mine was a normal life for someone from central Utah. Perhaps it's not. Looking back through all of it now, though, I know very well where the seed was planted that eventually grew into that torture session at the Marriott.

By 2011 I was in questionable health, with my bad back, and we needed money badly. The recession had hit the entire world, hard, and for an aging grandparent with health problems, it hit harder than most. Our savings were rapidly becoming depleted, jobs were scarce, and I began seeking for some kind of investment so that I could create a startup company.

I was afraid of losing my home at the time. We were behind on payments, and the bank was talking about foreclosure. As someone who had lost a home as a child, it triggered my insecurities.

A chat thread posted in some hackers' forum seized my attention by the throat and held on like a bulldog.

Well, this is intriguing. Digital crypto currency. It sounds like something out of science fiction.

Bitcoins, a digital international currency reportedly invented by a man named Satoshi Nakamoto in Japan, were still new to the world when I ran across them in March 2011. Very simply, the bitcoin system allows people to purchase products on the internet without intermediaries like banks or credit cards. Their purchases are recorded in a public ledger called the blockchain, but there's no central administrator or repository.

I've got to find out more about this, I thought.

Forum chats and links on one site, Bitcointalk.org, led to other sites like twists and turns in a digital maze. Or like ever-lengthening strands in some ethereal spider's web. The electronic conversations I ran across ranged all over the topic universe, from the fluctuating value of bitcoins and which online markets were using them now to whether Satoshi Nakamoto was an actual person.

Everything I read indicated that bitcoins were taking off, rapidly rising in value, though their use still seemed to be experimental. They didn't yet have a well-defined value compared to the US dollar or other prominent world currencies. Nor were they commonly used by well-known online retailers. Despite their theoretical versatility, examples of normal purchases by regular people still seemed few and far between, so when one appeared I pointed it out to Tonya.

"Look at this," I said, and motioned at a story glowing on my computer monitor. "Some guy paid somebody in Florida ten thousand bitcoins for two pizzas." I laughed. "That's what you call a three-hundred-thousand dollar pizza!"

In April, Bitcointalk.org ran a discussion about bitcoin mining. I dove into those chats like Captain Jack Sparrow after a loose keg of rum.

How do you do something like bitcoin mining? What does it take to get started?

I began to ask a lot of questions on the bitcoin forums. What kind of income could I expect if I did this? How long would it take to see it start flowing?

"There's really good money in this," I told Tonya. "It could make us rich."

"It sounds like another of your hare-brained ideas to me." She planted her hands on her hips and peered over my shoulder at my monitor, her expression skeptical. "How on Earth do you 'mine' for something that's digital?"

I chuckled. "It's not like digging for stuff. It's a record-keeping service. You verify payments, collect them into groups called blocks, and record them in the blockchain. The blockchain is sort of like a title to a vehicle, detailing all past owners and purchases. You get paid in transaction fees and new bitcoins."

Tonya puckered her brow. "It sounds like one of those video games where you go around collecting lost treasure or something."

On the surface it did sound kind of like that. But you used complicated algorithms instead of operating a controller with your hands. It was all about number-crunching, and the more that I began studying the numbers, the more I began to comprehend the beauty of the math.

I started bitcoin mining in April 2011 with the CPU I already owned. At that point, bitcoins were valued at only a couple of dollars each.

I joined a mining group in which several of us combined our efforts. It didn't matter if I found the block or one of the others did. Each of us received a percentage of the bitcoin reward based on the percentage of mining power each person contributed. For example, if I applied ten percent of the mining power, I received ten percent of the reward even if I hadn't found the block.

Working in a group made the payments more consistent. They came in daily instead of monthly or quarterly, as they would have if I'd mined on my own. I set up an account into which the payments were deposited. From there I could withdraw my bitcoins to my digital "wallet" and transfer them to an exchange for cash or trading.

"See, Tonya?" I said. "Income already."

By the end of the month, about the time three billion people around the world put their lives on hold long enough to watch Prince William marry Kate Middleton, bitcoin values had risen to over five dollars per coin.

"But what are bitcoins good for?" Tonya asked. "What can you actually buy with them?"

"Anything you can buy with money," I said, "if you can find retailers who accept them. It's like exchanging dollars for yen or euros when you travel overseas, except you cash in your bitcoins for dollars." I gestured at the TV, which at the moment showed Miss Middleton gliding up the cathedral's aisle. "You could even pay for a royal wedding."

Tonya rolled her eyes. "If you had enough of them."

I shrugged.

The bitcoin system evolved quickly in the following weeks and mining them didn't take long to overwhelm my CPU. By May I knew I needed to get a few Graphic Processing Units, or GPUs, to do my bitcoin mining. GPUs provide video capability, and serious gamers could purchase high-end cards that ran a few thousand dollars. I settled for some in the $700 to $1000 range. I didn't need them for video graphics, just the additional power and speed.

Especially the speed. My CPUs could only run mathematical equations so high. GPUs did it very well simply because it takes a lot of math to make graphics work.

I hadn't accrued enough bitcoins yet to buy GPUs with them, so the funds came out of our personal and family accounts.

Tonya stared at me when I told her. "You're spending *how* much for *what*? When are we going to start seeing some income from this mining business? So far all I've seen is a lot of outlay. And what about your real job?" She felt sure that the whole cryptocurrency thing was a scam.

My "real" job consisted of taking sales calls and monitoring a website for a nonprofit organization. To say it wasn't very demanding would be an extreme understatement, and my income from it was only $2000 per month, and my health was bad enough that I couldn't take on strenuous labor, so bitcoin mining seemed like an ideal source of income on the side.

The GPU cards were a pain in the neck to set up. I had to physically insert each one into a computer, pretty much like any other type of memory card, and then install the drivers and other software they needed to operate. Luckily, I'm good at that kind of stuff, but it took a lot more time than I expected.

With the GPU cards speeding up my computers, bitcoin mining sank its teeth into me like a rattlesnake. Tonya lost count of how many times she found me seated at my computer at the kitchen table in the dark. With the bluish glow from my laptop's monitor illuminating my face I probably resembled some kind of B-movie space alien.

"Come to bed, Curtis," she'd say with exasperation. "I'm sure the bitcoins will still be there in the morning."

At that stage, with bitcoin values so fluid, mining sometimes resembled playing the stock market. So, I did a little speculating too, buying when bitcoins were low and selling when their value rose. I also traded "arbitrage," in which I bought bitcoins at one site for a set amount, say four dollars, and then sent them to other trading spots with higher prices, sometimes a dollar or two in difference, maybe six dollars. Even with the transaction fees I still made a profit.

Yeah, I screwed up a few times. Sometimes I got impatient or nervous and sold my bitcoins too early. A couple of times I neglected to buy when bitcoins were low and would have been a good deal.

Tonya shook her head at me. "You've got to learn to hold onto them for a while," she said.

Between hours spent in the bitcoin mining groups, I still enjoyed joining chat forums to discuss the digital currency system. I branched out in my searches for online markets that accepted only bitcoins in trade, and especially for sites with chat forums.

That was when, late in May of 2011, while scrolling through forums on BitCoinTalk.com, I came across a thread talking about a market called Silk Road. It was a recent startup company, one that had only come online a couple of months earlier. After all the browsing and searching I'd done, they seemed to have the only forum dedicated to discussing bitcoins and mining. That and the online community surrounding it was my only interest, my true motivation. I was so excited, I felt as if I'd found myself a gold mine.

4: Into the Dark Web

Spanish Fork, Utah

No one is born evil, I suspect. Instead, each of us edge deeper into the darkness or into the light with every choice that we make. Viewed that way, good and evil are more directions than they are a state of being, and all of us, no matter how we see ourselves in relation to the world, can choose at any moment to change our course irrevocably. Unfortunately, I played around in the darkness too long.

I should've known there was more to Silk Road than it appeared when I discovered the only way to access the site was through something called The Onion Router, or TOR.

Developed by the U.S. Navy and employed by them since 2002, TOR is the digital version of Harry Potter's invisibility cloak, an encryption software designed to conceal both websites and visitors. It was dubbed "the onion" because of its multiple layers of security, which has led a lot of people in law enforcement to believe it's unbreakable. They believed that you couldn't trace users of the system. Whenever they tried, TOR would simply route them to a false address.

That, more than anything else, piqued my curiosity about the Silk Road site.

I've gotta check this one out, I thought. *Why are they so secretive? What have they got to hide?*

Disregarding the quiet but urgent warnings inside my skull and the prickles at the nape of my neck, I downloaded TOR to my MacBook.

That turned out to be the first of my challenges. It definitely was not a task for the average computer user. On a scale of one to ten, with one being downloading Safari or Firefox, I figured TOR fell in the four to five range. Loading it quickly became a case of "If all else fails, read the instructions." One step at a time.

Looking back on it, I think Firefox had the only TOR-capable browser. I had to disable Flash capabilities to prevent hackers from gaining access to my computer. I also had to disable Logging, which meant that none of my chats on forums could be saved. I wish that I had a lot of those records now.

Even with the TOR hurdle overcome at last, it took me two weeks to get into Silk Road.

Why isn't it accepting my password? Why won't it match my user ID? Has the site been hacked?

I didn't keep track of how many variations I tried. Forgetting my passwords from previous attempts didn't help either, which meant I had to come up with a new one for each additional attempt.

Finally, clenching my teeth with exasperation, I resorted to writing down the process, keystroke by keystroke.

Okay, I just pushed A. Now, click on this link. . . .

I still don't know exactly what got me through the door that first time, but I lapsed back in my chair with exhausted relief when Silk Road's login abruptly let me in.

Like a bud springing open, a page full of photos blossomed before my eyes, pictures of the products available on Silk Road.

That first time I didn't even pause for a glance. *How do you get to the forum? I want to see what people are saying about bitcoins.*

Silk Road Admin had decided the forum wasn't very good and so he created a new site, one separate from the market with a URL of its own. Ninety percent of chats there were about crypto currencies, things like the markets for bitcoins, their fluctuating values, and possible new developments in the digital currency arena.

Unlike the media's portrayal of Silk Road after DPR's arrest went public, not all of the chat was about buying, selling, and using drugs. When I kept track I found that only thirty percent of discussions seemed to be drug-related, and most of those were centered on marijuana and whether it should be legalized. Now it is legal in some states, though it wasn't at the time.

I did find a few people selling stuff through the forum rather than on the market side of the website. Some of the drugs they offered made my heart stop cold as a stone in my chest.

I should have known. Even with legal drugs, people can die if they don't know how to take them correctly.

I recognized them only because of the eight years I'd spent working as an EMT. A significant portion of my training for that had covered medications. Drugs to stabilize heart rates, drugs to stabilize blood pressures, drugs to relieve pain. When to use them, how much to use, possible reactions, and potential complications if used in combination with other drugs.

Even after leaving the EMT job I had continued to study the pros and cons of opium-based drugs. I'd received my disabling back injury during those years by catching my wife Tonya one day when she took a bad fall and I suffered from chronic pain as a result. Through searching out painkillers for myself, I developed a pretty substantial knowledge base. I certainly knew the boundaries between "safe" drug use and downright dangerous.

Some of these are in the hands of amateurs... I shuddered at the thought.

I didn't go back to Silk Road very often. Not even once a week at first. Every once in a while, however, I couldn't resist jumping on to see what was happening on the boards.

After a few visits I found that several new forums had been added, forums with different titles. They covered a variety of subjects, but none of them touched on the topic that sometimes woke me up cold in the night. So, in early June of 2011 I sent a private message, or PM, to Silk Road's system administrator.

"I've been checking out your forums for a while," I wrote. "What you really need is one for Health and Wellness, where people can post questions about the drugs they're using."

People *are* going to use drugs after all, legal or illegal, I reasoned. Some are self-medicating for pain or depression, others are seeking the thrill of a high.

With my EMT experience I knew I could prevent some of them from killing themselves by overdosing or endangering themselves in other ways. Maybe I could even help some of them get off drugs completely. All I could really hope to do was reduce the inevitable harm.

I didn't know if I'd get a response or not. Silk Road, I had discovered by then, was vast. I was only one occasional browser among thousands of regular visitors. Would Silk Road Admin give my suggestion even a cursory peek?

He did. "That's a fantastic idea," he replied. "Would you like to moderate the forum for me?"

That response triggered the psychological version of an adrenaline rush. More than a simple "Thanks for your feedback," more than just accepting my idea, Silk Road Admin had given me a rare personal affirmation, had acknowledged the value I could add to his empire, and had invited *me* to become part of it.

On reading his message I leaned back in my chair, stretched my arms over my head, and yelled, "Wow!"

Tremulous with excitement, I replied at once. "Sure, I'll help out. I've got some medical background. I'd be more than happy to."

Next thing I knew, Silk Road Admin had set up a new Harm Reduction forum and named me the moderator. That was the only place I answered questions about drugs.

Sometimes people asked for help with addictions or overdoses. Sometimes I got questions like "Is it safe to mix X with Z?" It was my job to make sure that members had all the right information.

Looking back, probably only twenty percent of my conversations on the forums were involved with drugs and harm reduction. The rest covered everyday stuff like what was going on in Europe where many Silk Road users lived, or election campaigns here in the States.

With so many points of view adrift among the Silk Road forums, conversations sometimes grew very heated, even profane. I noticed that especially when politics came up. When arguments rose, I had to step in to stop them and cool the antagonists down. Occasionally I had to ban certain people from the site for their belligerence, and then let them back on after they had cooled off for a while.

It was at this time that Chuck Schumer made destroying Silk Road a priority. On June 5, Schumer explained at a press conference that "Literally, it allows buyers and users to sell illegal drugs online, including heroin, cocaine, and meth, and users do sell by hiding their identities through a program that makes them virtually untraceable. It's a certifiable one-stop shop for illegal drugs that represents the most brazen attempt to peddle drugs online that we have ever seen. It's more brazen than anything else by lightyears."

And within a day, the Department of Justice opened an investigation into the Silk Road that became more and more intense over the next four months until it became a big priority.

Before long I realized I was spending ninety percent of my time each day on the forums, talking to people. Over time I made a lot of good online "friends." I had a lot more friends in the Silk Road forums than I did in real life, to be honest.

The need for my guidance in harm reduction was very real. There are lots of medications out there that are not controlled, but they're not approved by the FDA in the United States either. Silk Road could provide options for terminally ill people, giving them access to medications that weren't available in the US. Such drugs were also about a thousand times cheaper on Silk Road than they would have been at any American pharmacy.

A few weeks into the job, I found myself doing things like coaching Silk Road customers on the best way to snort ephedrine or steering them away from drugs I knew they couldn't handle.

Silk Road Admin knew I wasn't a vendor and I didn't take illegal drugs myself. He knew I was on the forums a lot, always around to help people out with even the most mundane questions. I coached many people through setting up generic computer programs. Things like installing Windows, for example. It was very basic customer service, and Silk Road Admin told me he'd noticed how I was always helping people on the forums.

I didn't moderate under my real name, of course. Since I know all about pain, due to that debilitating back injury, I chose Chronicpain to be my user ID for the Silk Road site.

When I'd been there a while, Silk Road Admin asked me to create a Wiki for the site. Another feather in my Silk Road cap, another boost to my self-esteem. I eagerly set about the task of building a basic Wiki, sort of a framework or shell that could be added to and fleshed out as needed later. Someone else, I don't know who, added a great deal of material to it after I set it up.

I explored the vendors' sites more often after becoming a moderator, and discovered Silk Road's full range of offerings. In those early days, most of them were completely licit—vendors from around the world offering good deals on everything from suits to lawn chairs.

But other things definitely lay on the shady side. There were a lot of soft drugs, but also cocaine, meth, and heroin. Probably porn, too. *No wonder this site was built on the dark web. No wonder it's buried under TOR.*

What's become known as the "dark web" has some distinct differences from its counterpart where most consumers do their shopping. The public web consists of sites you'll find with a simple search on Google, the businesses and organizations whose URLs end with .com or .org. Everything from well-known retailers and smaller businesses to churches and schools are accessible that way.

To my surprise, I learned that ninety-nine percent of the web is technically considered part of the "dark" side. Anything that uses the TOR program and whose URL ends with .onion is considered the "dark web."

While the dark web is known for nefarious uses such as child pornography and trafficking stolen personal information, the majority of its users are actually legitimate. For example, most news agencies use a form of it for their reporters to keep their stories from getting scooped.

Many universities have their own online infrastructure as well. It's not the dark web per se, but the principle is the same. Because their information isn't meant for public consumption, they require particular methods to gain access.

As I mentioned earlier, in the early 2000s the U.S. Navy came up with a way to prevent hacking by both foreign entities and the media, allowing the military to keep its communications secure and private. This is vital for national security as much as protecting their operations at sea.

The Onion Router, or TOR, works by bouncing and encrypting communications three times, making it very anonymous. One has to use the specialized TOR program, along with Firefox for the browser, to connect to the network. TOR URLs are very different from what you typically see online. They have names like 67dklweihosoieoij.onion, for example. Forget the "alphabet soup" for which the military is famous. This was pure "onion soup."

By the time I became a moderator, Silk Road's membership had swelled from fewer than five thousand when I first found it to a couple hundred thousand.

Contrary to what the government and the media wanted the public to believe about Silk Road, in that early phase the vast majority of its products and businesses were completely legal. One could simply find some really good deals there that weren't available anywhere else.

One example I remember was this guy from New York whom I'd met online, an American Jew who'd gone to Africa, though I don't know which country. He'd opened a gold mine, but his entrepreneurial spirit roamed in a number of different directions. He sold diamonds, gold, and clothing, among other items.

When he discovered that he could get $4000 suits for about $50 in the bazaars, along with very high-end shirts, we talked about going into business together. The clothing prices were so low because salaries for the people who made them ran at about three dollars a month. Sweat-shop labor, in other words.

Silk Road would be the ideal outlet for selling those suits and shirts, I thought. *Yeah, this is perfect! A site with that much traffic. . . .*

My working relationship with Silk Road Admin started slowly. Over time, however, as I was conscientious and prompt about answering questions on the harm reduction forum, and totally honest with people about the drugs they wondered about or were currently using, that relationship gradually gained momentum, like a freight train heading out from a station. Along the way I also assisted Silk Road

Admin with several small projects, purely as a volunteer. The man known only as "Silk Road Admin" seemed to appreciate my willingness to help out.

Through the months that followed I had hundreds of online "conversations" with him. Most focused on topics like our lives and families, but many focused on the political world at the time, his goals and aspirations for Silk Road, and what he hoped to accomplish through it.

I really liked him as a person. He was very giving, and plainly very intelligent. Besides that, I admired his long-term goals of making the world a better place. I thought he was genuinely trying to do good, sort of an online Robin Hood in a digital Sherwood Forest, especially since he claimed he wasn't running the website for the money.

You see, as Silk Road Admin put it, around the world, nearly all governments are corrupt to some degree or another. There are plenty of petty dictators who are genuine thugs, and in many countries throughout Africa, Asia, and Latin America, we have various mobs running things. A friend of mine once was in China, for example, and had been invited by a mysterious benefactor to tour the country to see about making a movie deal, but my friend got suspicious, so he asked the movie producer who acted as a guide, "I'm trying to understand. Is our host for this trip a bureaucrat, the Chinese mob, or a businessman?" The guide answered, "Oh, that is the great thing about China: In China, the government, the mob, and the businessmen are all the same people!"

Even in the best-run states, governments struggle to control their citizens—to restrict their speech and thoughts, to harvest their money, and control their personal lives.

So, my boss DPR seemed to see the people of the world as sheep, and the governments were simply trying to decide which ones to fleece and which should be taken to the slaughter.

Once people earned Silk Road Admin's trust, he proved to be very loyal to them, and very generous. I heard of several times when he gave money to people who really needed help.

Meanwhile, I continued my bitcoin mining. Cranking away with the GPUs, I started to see some income—not enough to pay off my house, but I was hoping to keep afloat until something materialized.

Also, during that time, partly because of my volunteer job as a forum moderator, I began to get acquainted with some of the Silk Road vendors--as well as you *can* "get acquainted" with anybody on the dark web, anyway.

I first connected with somebody called Googlyeyed when they responded to a message I had posted on the forum. I'm still not sure what prompted me to shoot a PM back to them, but we started chatting on TOR.

I knew Googlyeyed was a vendor but I had no idea what they sold until I checked out their site. Then I recoiled. I probably looked like a cartoon character with my eyes bugging out. *Man, they can't be doing that! Who the hell buys those kinds of research chemicals?*

While much of Googlyeyed's merchandise was technically legal, some chemicals were considered analogs to DEA "scheduled" drugs. Most drugs do have analogs, with names composed of numbers like NS-TV1 or some such. Drugs that fit into that class are definitely illegal.

To break it down, each of the major chemicals needed to make meth are harmless by themselves. It isn't until they're combined with other substances and cooked that they become dangerous. But if people can easily get all of those ingredients from one source, in the secrecy of their own homes. . . .

Later Googlyeyed added stuff like marijuana to the inventory, but I didn't recognize half of the products they offered at first. I just didn't know enough about chemical precursors for the hundreds of illegal drugs being produced around the world.

My qualms about the products didn't keep us from chatting. My wife would lie on the bed with me at night while I was on the forums, typing, and was privy to our conversations. We started with events taking place around the world back then, like the capture and death of Muammar Qaddafi in Libya, and an agreement between German chancellor Angela Merkel and French president Nicholas

Sarkozy to resolve the mounting debt crisis surrounding the euro.

"You must live somewhere in Europe," I said once.

"Why, yes, I do," came the reply.

I narrowed it down after a few more chats.

"The kids and I spent a lovely afternoon in the park yesterday," Googlyeyed wrote once. "We've had fine weather here of late."

And, "Two of my friends and I are going to lunch and then take in the Tate Modern tomorrow."

I looked up the Tate Modern with a little help from a different set of Google eyes.

Ah. That's one of the Tate Art Museums in London. I bet that's where Googlyeyed lives, and I bet it's a woman. Guys don't talk about doing lunch and checking out art museums with their friends.

Looking back, it seemed to me that the people I was working with felt very much like everyday people. Most of them were small users, but even the biggest drug lords were working from the comfort of their easy chairs.

We never chatted about Silk Road or what she sold. Frankly, I really didn't want to know. Still, it gradually became apparent that she had quite a network of her own, with people scattered all over the world. When she received an order, she bought the substance but had it delivered to someone on her team, and they shipped it to the customer. Because the item was never in her possession she was able to keep herself insulated if something went awry.

As with most of my chatting in the various forums, we stuck to talking about bitcoins, our families, and events taking place in our respective hemispheres.

We talked about *PGP*, which is a way to encrypt emails. PGP stands for "pretty good privacy." It was new at the time, but now it's a standard used daily by many corporate bigwigs. We chatted about the mundane stuff that comes up on any forum. With Googlyeyed it was rarely ever drug-related.

As our friendship and trust increased, I sometimes wondered if she wanted to draw me into her web, and not just from the business angle.

Meanwhile, Silk Road was expanding its own empire and morphing into something new, and more dangerous. . .

5: The Real Dread Pirate Roberts

Spanish Fork, Utah

When the DEA, FBI, Secret Service, and all of the other police agencies around the world began hunting for the Dread Pirate Roberts, they wanted a name, and in time they found it. But even today I have to wonder, isn't a person more than just their name? I think I know the Dread Pirate Roberts.

It's ironic in hindsight that while much of the merchandise available on Silk Road might be considered criminal, its system administrator declared "a strict code of conduct." Heroin was cool, but child porn was absolutely forbidden. There would be no fencing of stolen goods and no fake college degrees. He concluded his mission statement with "Our basic rules are to treat others as you would wish to be treated, and don't do anything to hurt or scam someone else."

Most of the people who first found Silk Road were techy types, people who spent a lot of time exploring the web and had a knack for it. That changed once the general public learned about it, thanks to the news media. Gawker, a web-based news outlet, ran a big story on it, which brought thousands of people to the site in June of 2011. After that we had visitors from every walk of life.

By the beginning of 2012, Silk Road had become more than an online marketplace. It had become a social spot for people who shared the same political beliefs. From there it evolved into a rallying point for like-minded individuals, those who desired to take power and control from an intrusive government and return it to the people.

A few leftwing nut-jobs showed up from time to time, but most customers were of the libertarian mindset, people who didn't want the government meddling in their private lives, and who believed everyone should have the freedom to do as they pleased. As long as one didn't hurt anyone else by his actions, why should the government get involved?

That was where the drugs came in, and why they ended up becoming so much a part of Silk Road's image. As time passed, more people did come to the site because of easy access to drugs. If someone wanted to use drugs and their usage didn't impact anyone else, Silk Road's administrator believed they should have that choice. I agreed with him on that, in a way.

One main tenet of Mormonism is that freedom is a basic human right. My ethical code is mine alone, and I don't try to force it on others. Mormon scripture warns against compelling others. We are taught that influence should only be maintained by "persuasion, by long-suffering, by gentleness and meekness, and by love unfeigned. . ."

So, for example, even though as a Mormon I don't drink alcohol or smoke cigarettes, I regard that as a personal health choice. I don't feel that I have the right to force others to conform to my beliefs.

The Mormon prophet Joseph Smith was once asked how he managed to control so many people around the world. He said simply that "I teach them correct principles and let them govern themselves."

Because of this, in part, Mormons tend to dislike big government. The prophet Brigham Young, for example, opposed the idea of having socialized education in the United States. Though Mormons tend to be some of the best-educated people in America, he feared that if people were taught that the government owed them an education, they would soon want the government to take care of them from cradle to grave.

So, while I'm not a libertarian, exactly, I think I can sympathize with them to some degree.

As the Silk Road site grew, the operator of Silk Road became more than just a system administrator to those of us who frequented its forums and marketplaces. He became the invisible leader of his dark web-based libertarian movement and a self-proclaimed "advocate for individual liberty." He openly declared his desires to "change the world." He told me about how he wanted to drill wells in Africa so that he could get clean water to villagers, and how he wanted to open orphanages there. He wanted to feed the hungry, clothe the naked, and put roofs over the heads of homeless people here in America. His ideas sounded as grandiose as they were noble, and while Silk Road was making a lot of money, he hoped to use it for the good of others. I'll talk more about this at the end.

In February 2012, having expressed his need to establish an identity in order to become a "true leader," he ran an explanatory post on the site and held a contest. "Who is Silk Road? I am Silk Road, the market, the person, the enterprise, everything," he wrote. "I need a name."

A week or so later, Silk Road Admin announced the winner: "Drum roll please... My new name is Dread Pirate Roberts."

Somebody nicknamed Variety Jones, whose real name turned out to be Thomas Clark I learned much later, submitted the winning name. I didn't make the connection to *The Princess Bride* at first, but then it gave me a good chuckle.

The new persona deepened the mystique surrounding Silk Road's owner and administrator. The moniker carried many layers of meaning, much like the pirate character in the movie, and even more like TOR security, which concealed his site. In fact, the name gave rise to kind of a cult of personality.

For the sake of brevity, Dread Pirate Roberts usually went by DPR, at least among those who discussed him and his marketplace on the forums. He began to post more often and with increasing urgency, like someone stirring the coals and fanning the nascent flames of revolution.

That was exactly what he intended.

"Stop funding the state with your tax dollars," he wrote once, "and direct your productive energies into the black market."

He considered every purchase from Silk Road to be "a step toward universal freedom" and "a direct challenge to the very structure of power."

Some participants on the forums began to wonder if there might be more than one man operating behind the name. Or was DPR schizophrenic?

The theory emerged because his personality seemed to shift from time to time. Usually he came across as an amiable benefactor, like a generous uncle or grandfather. Everyone on the forums knew how he'd provided one loyal user with the funds to buy a wedding ring.

On the other hand, he often seemed cold and compassionless when confronted with the consequences of the products he sold. I saw messages from distraught family members of people who'd died after using substances they'd acquired on Silk Road. DPR refused to make any kind of payment to them, claiming that the users had known the risks they were taking and he wasn't responsible for their fatal choices.

You never knew which DPR you might encounter from one day to the next. All I knew was that he was an exceptionally intelligent guy.

To this day I believe there were indeed multiple DPRs. The man behind the moniker claimed that there were, though he also claimed he'd given control of Silk Road to someone else. I don't believe that last part. At least I don't think that he ever gave the job over on a permanent basis.

To some degree, he would seek my counsel. If someone wanted to list an item on the site that we hadn't seen before, I might weigh in.

For example, one user once listed canisters of Russian nerve gas—NR2 on the site. While we did have weapons dealers on Silk Road, we had never had anyone try to sell weapons of mass-destruction. I told him, "No way are you selling that here!" and delisted it.

It seemed that every day brought a new moral quandary. We had one user who wanted to sell "donor organs" for example, hearts and kidneys and livers. DPR thought about it for thirty seconds and told the seller "Sure, we can do that." But shortly afterward he messaged me and asked my opinion, and I warned him against it. I mean, how do you know if those organs were really donated, or if they were stolen?

In fact, on one occasion, DPR wanted a break for a couple of days and floated the idea past me, asking if I would like to be DPR for a day, but we decided against it. Instead, he just took the time away.

But it may be possible that someone else acted as DPR on a couple of occasions.

Between moderating the harm reduction forum for Silk Road, I pressed on with bitcoin mining. The bitcoin system continued to expand and advance, and by early summer of 2012 it became clear that my GPUs were no longer adequate for the job. So in June I upgraded again.

I learned that Butterfly Labs was in the process of developing Application Specific Integrated Circuits, or ASICs, just for bitcoin mining. ASICs are integrated circuits designed for a single purpose, such as operating a cell phone, a TV, or an eBook reader. Development of an ASIC for a single new task can cost a few million dollars.

I mentioned this to Googlyeyed in one of our increasingly frequent chats. "I don't have enough bitcoins yet to buy as many as I'd like," I told her. "I'll have to dip into our family savings."

"Why don't I help you out with one?" she wrote, and promptly gave me about $10,000 worth of bitcoins.

"I'm not going to just take that for free," I told her. "I'll give you a cut of the profits or something."

"No worries, I'm not fussed about it," she assured me. I could imagine her giving a dismissive wave with a long-fingered hand.

Butterfly's bitcoin mining ASICs came in different sizes. Using bitcoins I'd mined with the aid of the GPUs and more bank transfers from our family accounts, I shelled out for three large ASICs at about $20,000 each, or about 3200 bitcoins. Today those bitcoins would be worth about $30 million. I guess I've bought my share of million-dollar pizzas, too.

I also bought a dozen or so small ASICs that came at a cost of about $800 per unit. My outlay totaled approximately $75,000.

Butterfly promised delivery in October.

That meant a five-month wait for the ASICs to arrive. In the interim I purchased several FPGAs, or Field Programmable units, to speed up my mining process. FPGAs aren't dedicated to a single task like ASICs. Instead, they can be repurposed from one application to another with the installation of new software. That made them a lot cheaper.

I ended up buying thirteen of the small, black-metal FPGAs, also for about $800 each. Another $10,400 purchase on top of the previous $70,000 or so.

Each FPGA had a cooling fan in its top and a bright red light that glowed while operating. Lined up on the table among my bitcoin-mining computers, all of them whirring and blinking at random intervals, they gave the room the appearance of a mad scientist's lab on a low-budget sci-fi movie set.

Tonya greeted the news of my latest hardware investments with something less than enthusiasm. "Curtis, that was a *huge* chunk of our savings! How are we going to make that up?"

"The ASICs are my last purchases, I promise, Hon," I assured her. "It'll all be income from now on."

"Enough to pay for all of these things?" Tonya asked, jutting her chin toward my new computers. Her expression wavered between skeptical and furious.

I did some calculations. I was only making a couple thousand a month working part-time. I hoped that the mining would prove to be far more lucrative.

"More than enough," I said with certainty.

I'd been working on another project between bitcoin mining and forum moderating. I thought it would be cool to have a nice-looking T-shirt or baseball-style hat for Silk Road so I designed some, emblazoned with the website's camel logo.

When I sent photos to DPR via private message on TorChat, he responded with enthusiasm. "These are great! I've got to get some."

"I can send you some," I offered.

He demurred. "Thanks, but that would give away my identity. I'll order them on the site like everybody else."

With July of 2012 came the World Series of Poker in Las Vegas. I'm a pretty good player and I felt confident of my ability to finish in the money, but having just purchased the ASICs, we no longer had the means to make the trip.

I remembered the time DPR had helped a customer buy a wedding ring for his bride-to-be, and I gave it some thought.

I wonder if he'd stake me to play? I guess it wouldn't hurt to ask. The worst he can do is say "no," right? I'll never know if I don't ask.

I sent him another PM. "I'll even wear one of those new T-shirts," I offered. "I'll be a walking billboard for Silk Road."

"The World Series of Poker?" DPR replied. "Hey, that's really cool! Sure, I can stake you for three grand. Good luck, and make sure you send me a photo of you wearing one of those T-shirts."

Tonya went with me to Las Vegas and we had a lot of fun. While I competed, she played the slots and won a few hundred dollars.

Things didn't work out as well for me as I'd hoped. I played some of the smaller games, in which I did a little better than breaking even. I came out about $1000 ahead.

I wore my Silk Road shirt while I played in the main World Series tournament. Several people complimented me on it. Quite a few asked me what the camel represented. I didn't actually tell them about the Silk Road site, just said it was a logo design I was working on for a company.

Unfortunately, I made a bad bet near the end of the tournament and lost the majority of my chips. I finished at two hundred ten out of two thousand competitors, just outside of the big money.

I wonder what DPR will say? I couldn't help feeling a bit of trepidation. I'd seen his occasional dark side by then. *He floated me all that money, after all.*

I told DPR I'd come out a little bit ahead in the small games, but he didn't seem to care about my loss in the main tournament. "That's the breaks, man," he wrote when I told him. "You win some and you lose some."

I told him I would return the money, but he hadn't expected me to do that. "Keep it as a gift," he said. Still, I kept my head down for a while after that.

I concentrated on bitcoin mining, from which we were seeing regular income by then to Tonya's immense relief, though she didn't give up her job at the local 7-Eleven. I sold only enough bitcoins to survive, usually between one and two thousand dollars' worth each month. I also concentrated on moderating that health-and-wellness forum on Silk Road.

Somewhere along the line I offered the Silk Road T-shirts and hats on the website. I had announced them on the forums, so people were waiting for them, but I didn't like the advertising photos. They simply didn't appear to be good quality. I never got around to setting up the account to sell the shirts, and after a while people began to wonder what had happened to them. Eventually they were forgotten.

My ASIC machines weren't delivered in October as Butterfly Labs had promised. When I inquired about them, I was told the fabricators had screwed up on the power consumption and they had to go back to the drawing board. One engineer informed me that they had actually been off in their calculations well before the machines were sent to fabrication. I was told to expect delivery some time the following year.

Sometime next year? I thought. *That's pure idiocy!*

Tonya was especially dismayed. "How reputable is this company, anyway?" she demanded. "How do you know they haven't just taken our money and run?"

"Butterfly Labs has been around for years," I said. "They're a solid business."

I had no doubts about the company's reliability, but the delay did set back my plans to build our income and earn back the money I'd paid for the ASICs.

By August of 2012 I was aware that a lot of illegal trade was taking place on Silk Road. I salved my conscience by telling myself that as a mere forum moderator, I had nothing to do with anything being bought and sold there.

Still, I felt an odd tingle at the nape of my neck when in late November of 2012, a few weeks after Barrack Obama defeated Mitt Romney for a second term as president, I received an unexpected message from DPR. "I just want to let you know that your work hasn't gone unnoticed," he wrote. "I'd like to offer you a position."

If I had been thrilled when he accepted my idea for the harm reduction forum, it was nothing to the excitement that came with that message.

"Oh my gosh, Tonya," I said. "DPR just offered me a job! This isn't volunteer stuff anymore, it's for pay."

"What does he want you to do?" Tonya asked.

DPR sent me a job description. I was to work eighty hours a week in customer service, resetting passwords for users and mediating sales disputes.

Eighty hours a week? I arched an eyebrow at that. *How can something like resetting passwords possibly require double the hours of a normal workweek?*

I would also forward customer issues to DPR, if they weren't password-related, and let him take care of them. He would pay me $800 per week, in bitcoins.

Tonya and I talked about it briefly. Resetting usernames and passwords? Neither of us thought it was that big of a deal. Neither of us had any idea that doing such a thing was as illegal as some of Silk Road's inventory.

I really needed that money. I was only making $2000 a month on my part-time job, and this would give us another $3200. I'd be working like mad, but I've never been opposed to hard work.

As I thought about it, I realized that DPR had hired me precisely because I was a Mormon grandpa, as clean as can be. He wouldn't want a junkie, like some of the people on Silk Road.

Still, I felt compelled to call my brother Darren before I accepted the job and ask what he thought about me working as an administrator on a site like Silk Road. Was it a good idea or should I turn it down?

"What do they sell?" he asked first.

I'd been expecting that. With a glance at Tonya, who stood at my shoulder listening to my end of the phone conversation, I told him. I was completely honest about what I'd seen there, all the illegal drugs as well as the completely legal items like computers and high-end clothing.

Darren remained silent on the other end for so long that I'd begun to think we'd lost our connection. At last he said, "As long as you're not dealing or selling anything yourself, I think you're okay. I'd go ahead and do it."

His statement burned deeply into my mind. *Darren's got a good head about things like this. If he thinks it's okay, it must be. I'm good to go.* I peered around at Tonya and smiled.

Apparently, Darren didn't know about the illegality of resetting usernames and passwords, either.

DPR requested a scan of my driver's license.

The same warning prickle I'd felt a few times before about Silk Road coursed up the nape of my neck and the same quiet, cautionary voice whispered between my ears.

That would leave me exposed. My real name, my photo, my street address, while he jealously guards his invisibility.

I dismissed the warnings. Most employers do require an applicant's photo ID, after all, and a driver's license is the most common form.

As an official member of Silk Road's admin staff now, I took a new username, Flush. I wanted to keep my admin identity separate from the one who moderated the forum. "Flush" was a hat-tip to my poker habit. But I worried. Very often that which we find horrific becomes something that intrigues and excites us, until we embrace it. Was I becoming like the Dread Pirate Roberts?

I had just entered a new game, with stakes far higher than I'd ever dreamed.

6: My Typical Workday as a Mobster

Spanish Fork, Utah

Late November 2012

Jesus once warned his disciples: "Behold, I send you forth as sheep in the midst of wolves: be ye therefore wise as serpents, and harmless as doves." I always strove to be harmless. I'd have been better off working to be wise.

"Flush, I want you to meet Inigo," DPR wrote in one of our first TorChats after he hired me. "He'll show you what needs to be done and how to do it."

Inigo gave me that prickly warning sensation from the beginning.

"Here's how you reset passwords," he wrote. "We do a lot of that for people."

He tried to take me through the process step-by-step, but it became clear pretty quickly that he had no idea how to do it himself.

Looks like I get to figure this out on my own, I thought with a sigh.

"We handle customer service and we work with vendors," Inigo informed me. "Our biggest workload comes from vendors. It just never stops."

That, I would soon discover, turned out to be the understatement of the year.

Inigo and I spent a lot of time together on TorChat during that first week, until I got comfortable with the various customer-service tasks.

About the time he was supposed to start showing me how to handle vendor concerns, Inigo went AWOL.

"Hey, Inigo," I wrote, "we've got a vendor in Europe who needs help with a payment problem."

No answer.

"Inigo, there's this vendor in New Delhi. . ."

No answer.

Great. I get to figure this out by myself, too.

I routinely sat down at my computer at about 9:00 AM and found two or three thousand problems waiting for my attention. Usually I could take care of them in a couple of hours.

Only two to three hours to take care of this. Why did DPR hire me for eighty hours every week?

Most of it consisted of resetting user names and passwords, but we handled disputes as well. For example, sometimes we had buyers who claimed that they'd never received their purchase. There could be good reasons for that—misdelivered mail, government seizures, mail theft. And of course, there were cases where the users were just hoping to get free product.

I had to make a lot of decisions, figure out who was right and who was wrong. If the vendor had a perfect record and the buyer had a history of issues, I sided with the vendor one hundred percent of the time. If it was a bad vendor, I sided with the buyer. If the situation wasn't clear and I had questions about the reliability of both, I split it fifty-fifty.

I solved each morning's batch of problems, but when I came back to work around 6:00 every evening I'd find another few thousand queries filling Silk Road's queue.

I could tell when Inigo was online because his name would appear as logged in. I rarely saw it there.

Where's Inigo? Isn't he supposed to be working on this? Doesn't his job description say "resolves issues," too?

Let's be honest. The computer program really resolved the issues, not me, not Inigo. I just had to know what button to push. From there, the computer's programming decided how to handle it. The only time a human had to intervene was if, after a few weeks, one of the parties still refused to agree. Only then did one of us step in. I handled very few cases like that. I'm pretty sure I never saw as many as ten of them.

Meanwhile, I saw even fewer signs of Inigo. Not so much as a hair for days at a time. Teeth gritted, I'd sit down and spend another two or three hours clearing the fresh influx. Sometimes I got up in the middle of the night to check.

Sure enough, three thousand more. But they'll balloon to six thousand by morning if I leave them. No way I'm facing that many first thing in the morning.

Where the hell is Inigo? He's supposed to be working vendor support as well. The influx is constantly increasing and there's no end in sight.

Maybe this is why DPR wants me to put in eighty hours a week. He knows Inigo is useless so he hired me to fill the gap.

Often, I actually put in a lot more than eighty hours per week, but having to work with Inigo was the only thing I really disliked about the job. That was mostly because we received the same amount of pay, despite his regular absences that left all the work to me. I found myself clenching my teeth with irritation on an increasingly frequent basis.

Inigo, I quickly learned, had underlying problems like his own drug use. Once he actually had the decency to apologize. Sort of. "Yeah, I took some heroin," he said, "and I was nodding off for three days."

During that time, I saw the paternal side of DPR. He always expressed interest and concern in his correspondence with us. He always asked, "How are you doing? How was your day?" and seemed genuinely interested on the occasions when I opened up.

He tried to mentor Inigo. "Here's a little life lesson," he'd write. "This isn't for you, Flush, but since I took the time to write this up, you might as well read it. You might get something out of it, too."

DPR wrote very well. I suspected he had a college education. He clearly hadn't come from a background riddled with drug use. He wrote a lot about his parents and how they'd brought him up, including important lessons they had passed on to him.

He had the best parents in the world, he often said. They were very forgiving and they had taught him well. I felt his appreciation for his family in his missives to Inigo and me.

He's trying to follow their example with Inigo, I thought. Trying to save Inigo's job, and maybe his life in the long run. He's got a lot of tolerance.

Well, for some things. But you'd better not be a minute late or a minute early for a scheduled TorChat meeting.

"When I said nine o'clock, I meant nine o'clock, not a minute before or after!" he ranted. "What don't you understand about that?"

Another time, soon after I began to work for him, we received a customer service complaint from the sister of a guy who had died from an overdose of heroin he'd purchased from Silk Road. What I discovered when I investigated the situation made my head spin. The way the Silk Road site was set up, children could have purchased drugs from it.

"Perhaps that's a hair too much freedom," I suggested when I reported to DPR.

"THAT'S MY WHOLE IDEA!" he wrote back, all in capital letters. It rocked me on my heels as sharply as if he had screamed in my face. Then he explained, "Any constraints would destroy the fundamental concept. And, no, I'm not giving any financial assistance to the sister."

As I sat there, blinking from the textual onslaught and reeling with the contradictions, that warning prickle worked its way up the back of my scalp again.

What he's doing is wrong and deep inside he knows it.

Or does he? Does "freedom" override ethics in his view?

I've tried to warn him. What he chooses to do with it is his responsibility.

Once again, his Libertarian philosophy was coming out. I have known a number of libertarians who were Mormons, and I sided with a lot of their views, but I had my qualms. For example, the whole drug use thing. Can anyone really choose to use recreational drugs responsibly? If you consider it long enough, the drug user's arguments break down. Certainly, a mom or a dad who is squandering money or destroying their health through drugs isn't being "responsible" to their children, are they?

I came very close to quitting right then. I'd considered it before, truthfully. Though I'd had a good idea, even as a forum moderator, what was really going on, I'd never known the full extent of it until DPR asked me to be an admin assistant. Then I saw every email that came in.

One of them spun a sorry tale of how the writer's loved one had become addicted to drugs because of Silk Road. Though they went on to say they didn't know that for a fact, they did know that having drugs so easily available wasn't helping.

I don't buy that entirely. Silk Road was something of a matchmaker. It allowed drug users to shop for drugs anonymously. So, isn't the user ultimately the most responsible?

It wasn't the only message of that kind we received during the two months I worked as an administrator. At moments like that I seriously questioned myself.

What am I doing, working for an organization that destroys lives in the name of freedom? Addictions are a form of bondage. People are dying or their families' lives are being ruined.

I felt beyond my depth. I suspect that even if I were Aristotle, I'd have felt beyond my depth.

When I searched the site, I found that most of the products had odd names only those who knew drug slang would recognize and understand. Silk Road's online store was full of them. Of the terms I knew, only about thirty percent really were considered illegal. But what about all the names and terms I didn't recognize? How many of those names identified substances that *were* illegal?

Then there were the weapons sites. *When a person buys a "Personal terrorism kit," complete with weapons, body armor, and fake passports, doesn't it sound like they're planning to violate Libertarian ideals? Maybe Libertarianism is a load of crap.*

My uneasiness increased, but I sighed and once more squelched the guilt-inducing whispers swirling in my head. *That eight hundred dollars a week really is helping. At least I can catch up on the house payments.*

I guess my attempt to nudge DPR's conscience was the reason he didn't send me any kind of Christmas greeting a couple of weeks later.

He hadn't completely lost confidence in me, however. Soon after the new year began I received a message from him, along with the other Silk Road admin people. "You may be contacted by a guy called Nob," he said. "Make sure you help him out as much as you can. He's very computer illiterate."

That's weird, I thought. *DPR's never asked us to help a particular person before. This doesn't make sense. Maybe they've got plans to do business together?*

That was the only thing I could suppose. I learned a good while later that Nob had contacted DPR and inquired about buying out Silk Road. DPR didn't want to sell, so he asked for a billion dollars. Nob said he couldn't go that high, but Nob's interest in the site planted the seeds for trust and friendship between them.

Shortly after that, I got an alarming inquiry from DPR. He had an idea, it seemed: He wanted to know if I would be willing to receive drugs in the mail and then simply write new addresses on the packages and ship them out to others. In short, I'd be like a Walmart distribution center, bringing in large loads of drugs and then shipping them out to mid-level dealers.

I suspected that it had something to do with Nob, and I told DPR that I wouldn't feel comfortable with that.

He told me that I would have to. If I didn't do it, I'd lose my job.

But after that, he went silent and never broached the topic again.

I never did hear directly from Nob himself, but soon DPR sent us another message. "Hey, I want you guys to help me. Nob needs some help getting people to his site."

"I don't know how we can do that," I wrote back. I wasn't into online marketing, after all.

"Well, write up an advertisement and send it out," DPR instructed. "Here's the list of people to send it to." He had attached a list of names to the message.

I scrutinized the recipient roster, and that something's-not-right-about-this sensation resurfaced. A lot of names on that list were heavy dealers. "I'm not going to do this," I told DPR. "I'm just not going to do it."

The qualms I'd felt earlier had continued to increase, to swell, to beat at my brain. *All these hard drugs going through. It's a constant stream of them.*

Until I took the admin job, I'd been under the illusion that the drug traffic was limited to marijuana, over-the-counter meds, and other "soft" stuff. The increasing flow of the hard substances began to weigh on my conscience.

By working at this job for 80 hours a week, I was becoming immersed in the world of the dark web, and my initial shock to the drug sales taking place wore off to some degree, became more commonplace, but I remained... alarmed, deep down.

I asked DPR more about Nob, and he explained that Nob was a higher-up in the mob. I think that he used the term "Mafioso." I knew then that I really didn't want to help this guy, so I told him I was out.

DPR didn't "scream" at me through another message, as I'd feared he might for my refusal to write the ad. He replied, "Okay, I'll do it myself, then. When you get inquiries, send them directly to me."

I raised an eyebrow at that. *He's vouching for this guy? Yeah, that's* really *weird.*

Before long I heard from Googlyeyed via the forum. "DPR sent me this dodgy PM about some bloke called Nob."

It wasn't a statement as much as a question, I realized. What could I tell her about Nob? Only what I'd learned from DPR himself.

"Well, from what I understand, he's okay," I told her. "DPR says he's okay." Then I asked, "What did he have? What was in that ad?"

I already had some suspicions. DPR had run some details past me, which was what had prompted my refusal to write and send out the ad. He hadn't said anything else to me about Nob after that.

I could feel Googlyeyed's tension in her next message, a presence as tangible as my own suspicious tingles. "He offered a deal for fifty kilos of heroin. Fifty kilos, mind! Can you imagine? He said that if you choose, you can buy a five-kilo test to be sure it's good, but future orders will be a great deal larger."

"So, this Nob is going to move large amounts of product?" I asked.

"It would appear so," she wrote back. "And DPR made it quite clear that if Nob got screwed, or if the product isn't received, he will personally reimburse him."

I let out a low whistle. "Is it specifically heroin?" I tapped to her.

"That's right," Googlyeyed answered. "But heroin really isn't my thing."

"It's not mine, either," I agreed.

"This smells rather fishy," she wrote next.

"Yeah, I think it's kind of weird that DPR is helping this Nob person," I said. "All I know is that DPR is willing to vouch for him."

"Well, I don't want to have anything to do with heroin," Googlyeyed said.

I couldn't blame her. *What if it turns out that DPR is an undercover cop? What if this is a big honey-pot? The whole thing seems so strange.*

"I could use some cocaine," Googlyeyed said. The tone of her message seemed contemplative. "I think I'm going to run a test."

"Okay," I responded.

"And I'm going to send it to you."

I honestly thought she was joking. It seemed like her kind of humor. I tapped, "Yeah, just call me Pablo Escobar, like in *Scarface*, ha-ha." I added, "All I'm interested in are some cheap anti-anxiety meds. My prescription is way too expensive and I'm running out."

Yes, I suffer from anxiety, and it had worsened during the last few months. No surprise there, between the undelivered ASICs, my home foreclosure, my introduction into the dark web, and this ongoing thing with Nob, but mostly because of working so many hours on the Silk Road site. Singlehandedly—most of the time—I had to make sure *all* the questions were answered and *all* the passwords were reset. There was a lot of work to do and it never let up. Though the tasks themselves were easy, they kept me busy to the point that they had become strenuous.

The Silk Road was a burgeoning business and might handle ten thousand transactions a day.

"Anxiety? Now *that* I can help you with, dearie," wrote Googlyeyed. "How about a few Xanax pills to tide you over?" Xanax is one of the most common drugs to treat anxiety.

"Thanks." I gave her my mailing address.

The year 2013 was only a couple of weeks old when the box arrived from Googlyeyed.

That's a good way to start a new year, I thought. *Maybe they'll calm me down, ease all these nameless apprehensions, and help me focus.*

I had expected ten pills at the most. Instead, Tonya and I stared at several hundred unmarked white capsules nestled in the opened box. Probably closer to a thousand of them, I estimated.

"How do you know these are really Xanax?" she asked. "I don't trust her."

Tonya had been privy to our conversations and had disliked Googlyeyed from afar ever since she'd mentioned that she'd like to come to the States to meet me.

I'd never had a reason to distrust Googlyeyed, though I hadn't encouraged her visit, and I knew she trusted me, but it wasn't worth the risk. I sent a PM to thank her for the box before I flushed its entire contents down the toilet.

"There's something else you may like to try," Googlyeyed wrote. "It's called N-bomb. It's only illegal in Florida and Russia, and can be very beneficial as long as one doesn't take too much. Why don't I send you a sample?"

N-bomb? That's a new one. I've never heard of anything by that name before.

I spent several hours researching it, to be certain that it really was legal. Though it was, I had second thoughts about it. Some college student had died from taking too much of it, and some sites listed it as a powerful psychotropic drug that can be sixty time more powerful than LSD.

"No thanks," I wrote. *I really don't want to take any stuff like that.*

Googlyeyed replied, "It's on its way."

7: The Surprise Delivery

Spanish Fork, Utah

Wednesday, January 16, 2013

They say that "Happiness comes in small packages." So does dope, unless it comes in a big package.

A single knock at the front door startled me out of a phone conversation with Tonya. Tonya had gone to Kentucky to take care of our sick daughter, and we were embroiled in a serious conversation about how to handle it. I was home alone, sitting at our kitchen table. Our two Chihuahuas' instant barking in response to the knock completely obliterated what she'd been telling me.

"Max! Sammy! Shut up!" I shouted at the Chihuahuas. When their barking persisted I said, "I gotta go, Hon. There's somebody at the door. I'll call you back in a few minutes."

Movement outside the front window caught my eye as I rose from the table. *Just the mailman*, I thought, noting a U.S. Postal Service jacket as he hurried away.

Except that he also wore sneakers and khaki shorts.

Nobody wears shorts in January. Not here in Utah, anyway. I wrinkled my forehead. *And didn't Tonya say our mail carrier is a woman?*

When I opened the door, a large white van, parked caddie-corner across the street, caught my attention. The ladder hanging on its side suggested that it belonged to a painting company, but no logo, company name, or telephone number blazoned its blank panels.

I vaguely remembered seeing it there when I'd glanced out the window an hour or so earlier.

That's strange. Really out of place. And it's been sitting there for a while.

My gaze dropped to the doorstep. A standard USPS overnight box lay there, about the size of two large bricks placed side-by-side. It weighed about as much as two bricks too, I thought when I lifted it up.

I checked the return address first, on an Inkjet-printed label. I stiffened.

Nob? DPR's vendor in Baltimore, Maryland? Something's not right about this. Vendors never put their names on packages. I couldn't even imagine how he'd gotten my address.

I squinted at the postage sticker next.

What the hell? How could it be zero dollars and zero cents?

That familiar, suspicious prickle had spread across my scalp like spilled ice water.

As I studied the package, I realized that it looked about the size where it could be money—perhaps a couple of stacks of hundred-dollar bills.

This isn't anything I've ordered. Something's really off here. He's the guy who sells coke. What do I do with it?

Our garbage cans stood near the front door. I set the box on the lid of one and stepped back inside long enough to rummage through a kitchen drawer for a pen. All I could find was a pink ballpoint.

It'll have to do.

Pen in hand, I glanced up and down the street as I scooped the box off the garbage can lid. Nothing else seemed out of the ordinary. Just that unmarked white van across the way.

With some effort I printed RETURN TO SENDER across the box's front. The pen seemed to be almost out of ink, so I shook it down and wrote over my first attempt four or five times to darken it. I laboriously repeated the same instructions in three or four other locations on the box.

Then I tried to stuff it into our mailbox.

Too big. Now what do I do with it? Maybe I should call the police.

Still burdened with that itchy, something-isn't-right sensation, I set it back on the garbage can lid, went indoors, and plopped onto a kitchen chair.

What do I do, what do I do? Man, something's really wrong here. Do I leave it out there? What should I do with it?

It says Nob on the return address, and by the size of the box it could be. . . cocaine. . . or money.

I wondered if he had sent me a bribe for something. Perhaps so that I would do him a favor.

Oh my gosh, Googlyeyed and I had that conversation about Nob and cocaine. Didn't she know I was joking when I said that thing about Pablo Escobar and Scarface? I told her not to send it, I know I did. Why did she do it anyway?

She hadn't trusted Nob. Had they been talking about me?

Or maybe it was something else. Maybe it was the N-bombs she'd mentioned. Those were legal. Could she have sent some through Nob?

I should have left the box on top of the garbage can. Or better yet, inside it. I should have called the police.

Truthfully, I should have let it lie completely untouched on my doorstep, like the proverbial sleeping dog. In a thriller novel it probably would have been a motion-detonated bomb.

I didn't do any of the things I should have done. By the time I finished writing RETURN TO SENDER on it in fading pink ink, I had coated the box with my fingerprints. If it had been a bomb, the front yard would have been coated with little pink bits of me.

Is it really cocaine? I was supposed to be getting a package of that N-bomb stuff from Googlyeyed. But she wouldn't have had Nob send it. Would she?

Well, if it is cocaine I can always dump it.

I shoved myself up from the kitchen table. Max and Sammy had stopped barking by then, but they trotted after me to the front door.

The box lay exactly where I'd left it on the garbage can lid, warmed by the wintry, late-morning sun. Its snow-dampened cardboard steamed gently.

The apprehensive prickly feeling had subsided, but a little voice inside my skull made one last-ditch attempt to steer me clear of trouble. "Don't do it, Curtis."

I hesitated. Shot another glance at the apparently empty white van across the street.

That's so strange. Where are the painters, or whoever? What is it doing, sitting there all morning?

Blowing out an uneasy breath I collected the box, hefted it, and headed back into the house.

I carried the box to the counter beside the kitchen sink, the two dogs still at my heels, and retrieved a knife.

If it's not N-bomb, it's going straight down the drain.

The first thing I noticed when I pulled the package from the box was the brown scorpion logo stamped on it.

That's got to be some Silk Road vendor. This is getting stranger and stranger.

Nob, or whoever had really sent it, clearly took packing seriously. The bundle had been wrapped in heavy-duty brown paper tape with fine twine running through it. You know, the old-fashioned kind of strapping tape. I could barely force the knife blade into it.

I huffed and puffed as I worked my way through layer after layer of thick, sticky tape enclosing a bundle about the size of a football. I felt as if I was wrestling with the thing, as if it were resisting my efforts every inch of the way.

If this is what it appears to be, and if I ever get into it, I'm dumping it right down the toilet.

Several minutes later, still gnawing into one layer after another, I had a fleeting thought.

What if, when I get all the way through the tape, there's nothing in here? What if it's nothing but a wad of tape? What if the whole thing is a scam?

That thought annoyed me so much that I gritted my teeth and kept sawing at it.

Without warning, powder as white as a Utah ski slope burst into my face. It billowed in a small explosion, as if it had been under pressure and had erupted from my puncture.

I recoiled, gasped, and blinked furiously at the sudden burning in my eyes. I swiped at my face with both hands. They came away coated with powder. It probably appeared as if I had been baking something with a lot of flour, but my tongue began to go numb and my heart raced under my ribs.

Oh my gosh, this really is coke. There's got to be at least a kilo of it here, and I've got it all over my face, all over my hands. . . . What the hell do I do now?

I scooped the thing up and wheeled toward the bathroom.

I'll flush it. That'll be easier, it'll be faster. I've—

Boom.

8: Framed by Nob

Spanish Fork, Utah

The American Psychiatric Association says that the number of sociopaths is about 4% and rapidly growing. If twenty cops beat down your door, there's a good chance that one of them will be a sociopath. In my case, I eventually discovered, I got two!

More swift blows echoed the first, simultaneously from the front door, the back door, and downstairs. I heard footfalls thundering up the stairs and I froze, package in hand.

"Police!" a couple dozen voices screamed over each other. "Get on the floor!"

I had one split-second glimpse, on my way to the rug, of dark, masked figures clustered too close together to count and bristling with rifles, and the bright red dots of laser targeting beams all over me and the walls. I have no idea when I dropped the cocaine, or if I might have thrown it, but I no longer had it in my hands by the time my chest hit the living room carpet.

"Don't move!" somebody shouted. "Hands out where we can see them!"

As I cautiously stretched out both arms with my palms pressed to the carpet, a heavy boot came down on my upper back. Its sudden weight forced out my breath as a cough.

"Hold still!" a deep voice bellowed.

Three or four men crouched around me. I couldn't be sure of the number but I wasn't about to shift enough to check. I didn't want a boot on my head, too.

With quick, practiced hands they frisked me, thoroughly, then locked handcuffs around my wrists—those cinch-up plastic ones, like electrical ties. I couldn't hear my pulse in my ears for the cops' hard huffing, adrenaline-spiked breaths. Like a pack of rabid, panting wolves, I thought.

"Get his belt-pack," somebody said. "That's big enough to keep a handgun in."

I was wearing a brown camouflage belt-pack, the kind hunters use, made of a hard material like vinyl.

"That's all my money!" I protested from the carpet.

Hands scrabbled at the belt's catch and tugged it out from under me. A few seconds later I heard a low whistle.

"Lookit this," one of them said. "Cold cash. These are all hundreds, guys, still in the bank rolls with that purple tape. . . and bank envelopes. . . ."

Yeah, so like I'm dealing out of my house, with the money still wrapped up by the bank. I gritted my teeth with fury.

"Geez, he's got more than twenty grand here!"

"That's our life savings!" I said. "What the hell are you doing?"

The apparent leader of the SWAT team cocked a thick eyebrow. "Well, it looks pretty suspicious when you're wearing twenty thousand dollars in cash around your waist."

"Where else are you going to put your money when you don't have a bank account?" I asked. "You guys are taking all my money! This is all I have to my name, this is *it*. If you take it I have nothing, nada, *zero*."

I'd had a savings account before I bought the ASICs, though most of the money for those purchases had come from my bitcoin account. By this time, I had closed out the bank account.

Now, you have to remember that this was at a time when a lot of banks were failing, and I worried that the government insurance program on accounts might collapse. Plus, I was becoming more and more aware of just how much cybercrime is going on in the world, so I didn't trust the bank security.

At that point the SWAT-team leader took his man to the side. "We can't confiscate all of it," he said.

They didn't give my belt-pack back to me, though.

The mind runs in odd directions when under duress. All I could think was, *how am I going to pay the household bills without it?*

I have no idea how long they left me lying there on the floor. It could have been only two minutes, it might have been two hours. Time seemed to have completely stopped.

Nor did I count the number of times that heavy boot smashed down between my shoulder blades. It felt like being stomped on by a bull. I have no idea what I did that prompted the repeated blows.

All I could do was lie there and listen to what sounded like a Viking pillaging party rampaging through my house. I grimaced and winced at the noise of closets and cupboard doors banging, the scrape of drawers being pulled out, muffled crashes and bangs from bedrooms, and harsh voices reverberating in the hall.

When I closed my eyes for a moment, images of the walls collapsing and the roof being torn off careened through my mind.

Like that housefire in my teens, minus the flames.

My Chihuahuas Max and Sammy darted through the forest of boots and black-clad legs, snarling and snapping. I couldn't take my eyes off of them. I kept expecting somebody to kick one or the other across the room. Instead, I heard chuckles and exclamations laced with amusement.

"Hey, that little dog just bit me!"

"Yeah, he got me, too."

"Now that's what you call a real ankle-biter."

At one point, Sammy even jumped up on my back and snapped at the police in an effort to protect me.

Eventually, a voice rumbled somewhere above me, "Okay, we're going to lift you up now."

Large hands hooked me under my arms and hauled me to my feet. With my face and tongue still numb from the cocaine, I didn't realize I had blood dribbling from my mouth until I saw the crimson stain on my shirt.

I swayed until I got my balance. A couple of the men maneuvered me to the living room sofa, cut off my cuffs, and pushed me down on the couch. Despite my lack of resistance, the plastic bands had already dug into my wrists.

When I lifted my head, I found myself facing twenty or more men, all armed with M-16s, all studying me through narrowed eyes. For many of them, masked as they were in balaclavas, their eyes were the only parts of their faces I could see.

One man, clad in street clothes rather than assault gear, positioned himself in front of me and showed me his badge. "Carl Force, DEA," he said.

He stood roughly six feet tall. Bald but muscular, he exuded hardcore cop attitude.

Something stirred in my head. Conversations with DPR about his new buddy. The name on the box's return address label. It all clicked together. I looked Agent Force in the eye and said, "Hi, Nob."

The name Nob is a derogatory term used in England for the word penis, sort of like "prick" or "dick." I suspect that he knew that.

He appeared startled for about half a second before he said with great indignation, "I'm not Nob."

"Oh, bullshit. I know you're Nob."

"No, I'm not," Force repeated. "I'm in constant communication with him, but that's all."

It seemed pretty obvious to me. I shrugged. "Whatever, Nob. I wasn't born yesterday."

It also seemed obvious that he was the one who had sent the cocaine.

"Listen," Force said, "we, the DEA, have been collecting information on you through multiple sources. Granted, Nob was one of them, but that's not me."

As if to prevent me from speaking again, he abruptly asked, "Mr. Green, you know you have the right to remain silent, don't you?"

I don't know whether I said, "Yeah," or simply nodded.

A shout from another room interrupted him. Most of the men scattered. Agent Force ordered, "Stay right there."

"I'm not moving, Nob," I said.

It wasn't until later, when my mind had cleared, that I realized he he'd never read me the whole Miranda. He never came back to finish.

Little Max, the older of our two Chihuahuas, watched me from between the milling jackboots. His already protuberant eyes practically bulged from their sockets and his whole tiny body quivered with terror. Under normal conditions Max was notorious for being a biter, but he stood there whining and whimpering and mincing in place as only very small dogs do.

With the doors broken open, an icy winter wind blew through the house.

"Can I pick up my dog?" I asked through numb lips.

"Go ahead," somebody said.

When I bent to gather Max from the floor, Sammy jumped up on the couch as well, still prancing and whimpering. I held them both to my chest and felt them shaking. They yipped and licked my face but their trembling began to ease.

For the next while, I really don't know how long, I sat there dazed and in shock. Maybe the cocaine was having its way with me, too. I wondered if the package had been rigged to explode, with something like a dye-pack.

It's hard to describe, thinking back. I felt no anger, no fear, just a numbness that had little to do with cocaine hitting me in the face. I felt as if I wasn't really there, as if I was adrift in some surreal waking dream.

I could hear them still searching the house, though most of the crashing and banging had subsided by then. Occasionally I made out whispers or low-voiced mutters, even a chuckle or two, but I couldn't understand what anybody said.

"Got any guns or knives that we need to be aware of?" a rough voice queried from behind a balaclava.

"I gave them to my daughter," I said through my dry mouth. "She's got them all at her house."

Speaking brought the iron taste of blood to my tongue. As a former EMT I knew very well what that meant. *The guy who stomped on my back, Nob, ruptured a bunch of capillaries in my lungs.*

It'll stop, I tried to reassure myself. *That kind of bleeding doesn't last long.*

That was my only coherent thought for a while. I simply sat there trying to comfort my quivering dogs and listening to the ongoing human tornado wrecking my house.

At one point one guy flung a bundle of priority mailing boxes at my feet. "Why do you have all these boxes?"

That roused me from my daze. "Our other daughter is in Alaska. My wife got them before Christmas to send her packages. She ordered the boxes and they ship them to you, so she ordered a couple of sizes. . . ."

I realized I'd lapsed into rambling.

"Do we need to bring in the dogs?" I heard one SWAT guy ask his commander. "Is there anything else?"

I didn't hear the response called from another room, but the guy twisted to address me. "Do you mind if they bring some drug-sniffing dogs in?"

I don't have anything in the house. Should I make them go through hell?

I hesitated before I answered. Another memory had surfaced. We'd had some foster kids fifteen years earlier who had smoked marijuana. *Who knows what they might have hidden in our house?*

We knew they had smoked pot all the time. In fact, once when Tonya and I were looking around after they left, we found a little pipe. Though it had been empty and appeared to be brand new, I couldn't help thinking, *Oh, man, can you imagine if they found that?*

Finally, I said, "Go ahead and do it. Look all you want. I don't have anything to hide."

They never did bring in any K-9 sniffers. I guess somebody believed me.

It wasn't until days later that I fully realized what I'd done during the distress of the raid. My methadone prescription limits me to four pills a day. I took six of them while the raid was going on around me.

It's a miracle I didn't get myself in medical trouble with that!

A guy wearing a U.S. Postal Service jacket planted himself before me. Yeah, the same guy in sneakers and khaki shorts I'd glimpsed trotting away from the house earlier. He stood there with his pale, skinny legs apart like some god from Olympus, planted a fist on his hip, and flashed his badge at me.

"U.S. Postal Inspector," he said, in a tone that suggested I was supposed to be impressed. "You might as well come clean, Mr. Green. We know a lot more about your little operation here than you obviously think we do."

I felt sorely tempted to say, "Only if *you* explain why you left that box on my doorstep," but I didn't think that would be prudent with a couple of rifles still pointing at my chest.

Instead, I said, "I didn't order that box." I nodded toward it, still lying on the floor where I'd flung it.

My guards exchanged knowing expressions. "Oh yeah, right," one of them muttered.

"Have you ever ordered anything from Silk Road?" Mr. Postal Inspector God asked.

"To be honest," I said, bouncing the dogs, who had begun to bark again, "I have ordered a couple of things, but what I ordered wasn't drugs, and I haven't received anything."

I paused for a few moments to consider. "Well, I take that back. The first thing I ordered was described as pain pills. I can't remember what they were called, but I saw them for sale and thought I'd try them. The internet said that they actually worked, so I paid for them, but I never got them."

My guards exchanged sly grins. I could imagine the wheels turning in their covered heads.

They're thinking, 'This guy orders a kilo of cocaine. He must be a real bigwig in the distribution chain.'

Mr. Postal God put his mental speculations to a question. "So where are you selling and shipping this stuff?"

I gaped at him. "I'm *not* selling. I haven't shipped anything! I don't do that. What are you talking about?"

They have to know that I've been framed, don't they? I didn't order anything.

Postal God leaned in at me. "Don't bother trying to play dumb, Green. You've got a kilo of premium coke scattered all over your carpet and a stack of priority mailing boxes which, for some reason, weren't used to ship Christmas presents." His tone grew sarcastic as he jerked a thumb over his shoulder at the pile of boxes flung on the floor. "We're all quite capable of simple arithmetic."

I shook my head. "I *didn't* order that coke. I have no idea where it came from." *Actually, I have a pretty good idea.* "And I certainly don't sell it."

Behind the Postal God, half a dozen brawny SWAT guys in full battle-rattle lugged our huge gray safe into the living room. They had hauled it from downstairs, so now their huffing breaths came from exertion rather than adrenaline. They dropped it with a floor-shaking thunk.

"Do you mind if we open this up?" one of them said through his panting.

It once had a combination and a key, but I said, "I haven't been in that thing for seven or eight years. I have no idea what the combination is or where the key is, so it's no good to me."

I heard a few balaclava-muffled mutters.

"Take it outside. . . ."

"Anybody got a heavy-duty saw?"

They hefted it with a grunt, manhandled it through the mangled front door, and dropped it in the snowy yard where I could see them through the window.

Somebody retrieved a heavy saw, and I watched them go at it. A couple of them took turns, and their collective breaths formed a vapor cloud about their heads.

I couldn't help remembering Geraldo Rivera opening his mysterious vault on live TV several years earlier, after building speculation and anticipation in his viewing audience for a couple of weeks. I also couldn't help feeling rather curious about what my safe might really contain.

I wonder what I did have in that thing? Or is it as empty as Geraldo's?

Apparently, one of the neighbors got the whole thing on video because I learned later that the little drama in my front yard made the local evening news. More cops had been at the house than I'd known, so that the street was lined with black vehicles, an ambulance, and a firetruck. I'd only seen maybe a little over a dozen officers, but it sounded as if a lot more stayed outside. I learned that when the cops first hit my door with the battering ram, all three of them got knocked back on their butts. It was a good, solid door. It held them out, even though it was completely unlocked. They could have turned the knob.

Meanwhile, Mr. Postal God never let up on his questions. Or rather, on his efforts to coerce me into confessing that I was indeed a major-league drug-dealer. At one point he said, "Now, if I were to take your picture around to the post office here in town, would anybody recognize you?"

Does he mean on a wanted poster? What an idiotic question!

"Well, yeah," I said, struggling to keep the sarcasm out of my voice, "the local post office definitely would recognize me. I've lived here for twenty-five years. They'd better know me after that much time.

"In fact," I added, and lapsed into weary rambling once more, "I have a business account at the post office. I had to go over and put my name on it, my business name. I've had it there for the past year or something. But I haven't had one piece of mail come to us...."

Eventually the SWAT guys who had dissected my safe all trooped back indoors, slump-shouldered, and with disappointment showing in what little I could see of their faces.

"Well?" demanded Mr. Postal God.

"Nothing," sighed the SWAT guy with the saw, "except a few dead bugs."

That's all Geraldo found in his vault, too.

Some thoroughly stressed bit of my psyche wanted to give in to maniacal laughter. I didn't let it.

The postal inspector's interrogation continued until a shout came from the kitchen. "Hey, gents, I need you to bring Mr. Green in here." I wondered what new surprise they had for me.

9: Busted Doors, Busted Lungs

Spanish Fork, Utah

Most of what I believed about cops, I'd learned from watching police dramas. The cops are always the good guys, searching for justice, right? But what we see on television is a distortion, a carefully crafted illusion that some people believe is created in an effort to condition us to not see the world as it is. By dividing the world into cops and robbers, we delude ourselves.

One of the guys who'd been left to guard me reached for my arm. I struggled to my feet, still clutching Max and Sammy. He marched me into the kitchen.

Agent Force stood beside the table in front of my open Mac Book Pro. Another guy in street clothes, evidently a computer technician, busied himself with downloading everything I had set up on the table, including my bitcoin-mining computers and my cell phone.

That's a total waste of time and energy, I thought. *There's nothing of interest on those.*

Of course, they probably have a different definition of what constitutes 'interesting' than I do.

While most of the break-and-enter team gathered around, including a couple of officers from the Spanish Fork Violent Crimes Unit, Agent Force jerked a thumb in the direction of the laptop's monitor. "So, you're an administrator on Silk Road, eh?"

I couldn't keep myself from thinking, despite everything going on—or maybe because of it—how appropriate the name "Force" was for a guy who had *forced* his way into my home, my business, and every other aspect of my family's privacy. Maybe a little too appropriate, in fact.

Is that really your name, Carl-Nob, or did you come up with that yourself?

He directed my dazed attention to the laptop squeezed among all the other hardware on the kitchen table.

I had been logged in with everything open when that knock came at my door, and I hadn't closed anything down.

Not even TorChat. I would've been an idiot to deny it. My screen name, Flush, appeared right there on the Silk Road site, identifying me as an administrator as it always did when I logged in.

"I told you I was," I said. "Moderator, administrator, they're all the same to me."

Force gave a "Hmph" and said, "This is what I want you to do, Mr. Green. I need you to come over here and sit down at your computer."

The technician must have been finished with what he was doing because he slipped away, leaving the chair open for me.

I saw at once what had caught Force's interest. Sometime during the last half an hour, most likely in the middle of the mêlée, Googlyeyed had popped online.

"We need you to do a little chatting for us," Force said. "There's somebody on here that I suspect you know." He sneered, "Boy, if I see any transactions in here about you being a dealer, your ass is grass."

Right, Nob.

"I know," I said, a lot more calmly than I felt. "Go ahead, look all you want."

I set Max and Sammy down, dropped onto the kitchen chair, and reached around the laptop to pull it within easier reach.

Three SWAT gorillas jumped in. Two seized my hands, one from each side, while a third guy probed around and under the laptop.

"What the hell?" I demanded.

"Just making sure you don't have a knife or handgun stashed under there," one of them said through his mask. "We don't take kindly to getting stuck or shot."

No kidding, I thought, followed by, Like I'd really try something. One of me versus all of you. That'd work out really well. I've been stomped on enough for one day.

When they finally allowed me to put hands to keyboard, I asked, "What do you want me to say?"

Thinking back, I should have said, "Why don't you guys sit and talk to her? I'm not gonna do it because whatever I write will be implicating myself." In my rattled state I went along with it.

"Tell them you got the stuff," Force coached me. "Say something like 'Great news, package arrived today,' or 'Good news! I got the package today.'" He shifted in closer to watch over my shoulder while a dozen more assault guys, rifles still balanced in their hands, crowded up behind.

TorChat looks like the chat browser of any social media. Think exchanging PMs on Facebook, for example. There's nothing visibly unique about it.

"Okay." I obediently typed out every word he dictated to me. "Hey, Googlyeyed, great news! I got the package today."

It was a coded communication. I knew that. Payment was never released to any Silk Road vendor until the purchaser acknowledged receipt of their order. My innocent-sounding sentence basically informed Googlyeyed, "I got the package, you can release the money to Nob now."

I glanced sidelong at him. His expression never altered. Not so much as a flicker around his eyes.

Within moments a reply appeared. "Oh, fantastic! Good to know it arrived."

I heard the shuffling of booted feet at my back as several SWAT goons tightened the circle about me. They all peered over my head at the monitor. A few of them grunted "Huh!" in a manner that might have translated to "Yeah! All right!" had they been capable of normal human speech. I didn't peek around. As tight as they stood, I could literally feel them breathing down my neck.

I couldn't see Force's reaction, however, so I twisted in my chair to eye him. "That was not a natural response for me," I told him. "If it'd just been me writing this, I'd be like 'What the hell did you send me?' That's what I would have said."

Force shrugged. I had shifted enough to see that. "Just say what I tell you to," he ordered.

I worried that he was trying to implicate me in a crime, as if I'd ordered the stuff.

I felt the steady gazes and eyed the hard, inscrutable faces clustered around me: Secret Service men, Homeland

Security toughs, DEA Agent Force, two or three local cops, and Mr. Postal Inspector God. A chill coursed up my spine that had nothing to do with the January breeze whipping in through my sagging front door.

While we all watched, another message from Googlyeyed materialized on my monitor. It was clearly a question, but I had no idea what it meant.

The whole crowd of house-crashers fixed their collective gaze on a particular individual, a big man with a shaved head, and a variety of colorful tattoos across his neck and up his arms. Obviously an undercover cop.

"Joe?" Force asked, indicating Googlyeyed's question. "Any ideas?"

Mr. Undercover nodded curtly. "It's a street term, Carl. Basically, they're asking what the product stamp looks like."

I remembered the scorpion logo I'd seen on the wrapping inside the box but I held my tongue.

Saying anything probably would only incriminate me further in their eyes.

"Didn't notice," somebody muttered, and shouldered his way out of the mob. A few seconds later—I could hear my racing heartbeat in my ears during the taut, ensuing silence—the guy announced from the living room, "It's a red dragon."

"High-quality Peruvian," somebody behind me murmured.

A red dragon? It looked more like a brown scorpion to me.

"Tell him that, Green," Force said, jabbing at my monitor.

I typed it out. Everybody went quiet again, waiting.

"Fantastic!" Googlyeyed replied once more.

"Okay," Force said, his voice calm and deliberate. It appeared that the single word had confirmed something to him. He motioned at one of the guys who'd been guarding me. "You can take him back to the living room now."

I peeked back once, scanning for Max and Sammy among the table legs and heavy boots, as the armor-clad Homeland Security gorilla marched me to the couch. Agent Force had taken the chair in front of my laptop and now sat far forward, eyeing the monitor from beneath scrunched brows. Its bluish light gleamed from his bald head.

In another minute or so, Force followed me into the living room. "You'll be booked into the Utah County jail," he said, and slapped my cell phone into my hand, a first-version Samsung Galaxy with a slide-out keyboard. "The second you get out, I want you to call me. Do *not*," he emphasized with a threatening glower, "talk to representatives from any other agency that may try to contact you. Call me if you do hear from anybody else, got that? The only person you may talk to is Secret Service Agent Shaun Bridges."

I barely heard him. All I could think was, *Jail? I've never been in jail in my life.*

Later I would wonder why he'd wanted me to talk to only him or his friend Shaun Bridges. Weren't they from different agencies?

Numbness set in once more. I merely nodded.

Two or three guys began to mutter behind me. I overheard bits and pieces of their conversation.

What were they going to charge me with? Possession of a kilo of cocaine. Yeah, definitely that. But they couldn't charge me with intent to distribute, I imagined, because I didn't have any scales, any baggies, none of the usual dealer paraphernalia.

"So, what's the bond for something like this?" one of them wondered aloud. He stood there holding my belt-pack, the first time I'd seen it since they'd pulled it off me.

"Look, you guys," I said, "you took all my money. I'm not going to be able to bail myself out."

They stared and stared at me as if they'd forgotten I was in the room.

"Twenty-five hundred should cover it," said the apparent guy in charge.

I was afraid that was low. I mean, if I were a big drug dealer, wouldn't there have been hundreds of thousands?

"Fair enough," someone said. I suspected they knew that I wasn't guilty.

A Homeland Security man in the group counted out a wad of crisp bills. "I need you to sign for this, Green." He brought up a form on his iPad and shoved it under my nose.

"You're making me sign to get my own money back?" My tone carried my incredulity.

He favored me with a warning expression. "Look, we really don't have to give *any* of it back to you, you know."

I signed for it.

What'll it be next, my bitcoin mining computers? I've got fifteen thousand dollars' worth of equipment sitting there on the kitchen table.

As if he'd read my mind, the HSI guy added, "You know we could take all of that, too."

"How can you take that away?" I demanded. "There's nothing illegal about it."

"Technically, we could confiscate it," he said, "but you lucked out. We're not going to."

"Put him in the car, let's get going," someone barked from the battered front door.

I finally balked. "You shouldn't take me in," I blurted. "I'll be much more valuable to you if the Silk Road operators don't know you've arrested me."

I reasoned that DPR would cut me off as soon as he found out I'd been arrested. I wouldn't be able to help the government track him or shut down the site if I couldn't get on it anymore.

One guy snorted behind his balaclava. "They won't find out," he said.

Somebody else added, "We're smarter than that, Green. This is our job, after all. We know what we're doing."

I suddenly remembered DPR's request for a PDF of my driver's license. And I remembered the ads for hit men on Silk Road. There was no one thing that made me worry, just dozens of little things. "You don't understand. He knows everything about me and he's got millions of dollars. Making my name public is a potential death sentence."

I heard more snorts, and a dubious "Huh" from a few.

The officers from the Spanish Fork Violent Crime Task Force closed in as if I was the kind of guy who'd rape women and murder children.

I hardly had time to whisper a comforting word to my dogs, and worried whether they would be all right.

To my surprise, they actually seemed apologetic about putting me in cuffs again. They waited to do that until after they'd loaded me into their car. An unmarked undercover car. No lights on top, no city or county logo blazoned across its sides. To my even greater surprise, they put me in the front seat rather than stuffing me into the back.

"Man, I'd prefer not to take you in," one of the cops said, "but if we didn't and the feds found out, we'd lose our jobs."

Like the home-invasion force they used plastic cuffs, but they put my hands in front of me this time. More practical for sitting in the car, and certainly more comfortable.

Only then, for the first time since all the banging and bodies crashing through every door in my house began, did I no longer fear that I might crap my pants. My spine and ribs ached from the repeated stomping on my back but my heart rate began to slow and my breathing began to steady.

"What's this Silk Road website Agent Force was talking about?" one officer asked. "How did you become an administrator for it?"

I described it in detail. "It's not all drugs, though there is a lot more of that now. They've got vendors who sell things like computers, precious metals, you name it."

"So, you can get Mac computers and stuff for a discount on there?" asked the other man. "Maybe I'll get on and look around a little myself, see what I can buy."

"How did you discover Silk Road in the first place?" the first guy asked.

I told them about bitcoins and bitcoin mining, and how my search for businesses that accepted payment in bitcoins had led me to Silk Road.

"That sounds really cool," said the younger guy. "Where can I find out more about that?"

We drove through the winter landscape, brown dead fields with snow, and majestic white mountains so close that you almost felt like you could reach out and touch them.

By the time we arrived at the Utah County jail, not too far from where I lived, things had begun to feel more normal. I no longer felt like a prisoner of the war on drugs but more like I was going on a ride-along, hanging out with a couple of longtime law enforcement buddies. My heart rate had returned to normal and my palms had stopped sweating.

Some of the tension returned upon entering the booking center. The women at the front desk eyed me through scowls that might as well have shouted, "What a scumbag!" and they spoke to me with a terseness that reinforced the impression. No one appeared friendly. I suppose that's what comes of working day in and day out among the shadier members of society.

They think I'm one of those shady types, too.

When some guy in the booking center saw my belt-pack and found what remained of my money he said, "Twenty-five hundred dollars? What is this, evidence? You can't keep it, you know."

One of the officers who'd brought me in interceded. "No, sir, that isn't evidence. This is Mr. Green's personal money and yes, he's allowed to keep it."

I felt a rush of gratitude for him.

The booking guy grumbled. "Not in the cell, he won't. We'll have to secure it here and he'll have to sign for it when he's released or transferred."

I allowed myself a breath of relief, and coughed up more blood. *I thought that would've stopped by now.*

The worst was yet to come.

10: On Becoming a Fish

Utah County Jail

In a jail, a fish *is a new inmate. They're called that because they move about like minnows in a school, timidly lurching this way and that in small groups.*

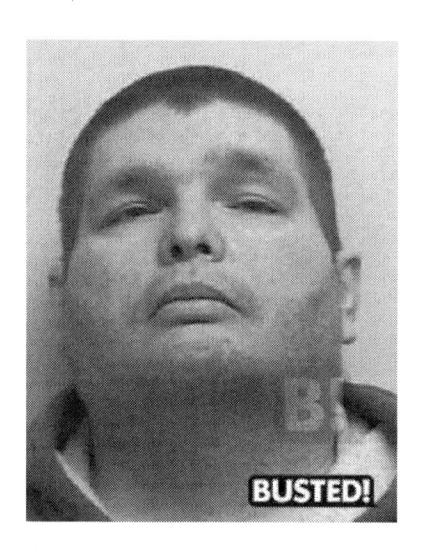

What followed was everything I'd ever seen in a cop show, but somehow different. Since I'd never been arrested before, never even got a traffic ticket, I really didn't know what to expect, so I found it all to be very interesting. They lined me up to a wall with a painted measuring stick to show my height, handed me a small board with my name spelled on it in removable black letters, and took mugshots, front and profile. They didn't have to tell me not to smile.

They questioned me. Nothing about my alleged crime right then, but they seemed to want to know every detail of my life from the moment of my birth. Where were all the places I had lived? Where did I work? Was I married? What was my Social Security number? Driver's license number? What kind of tattoos did I have? How about birthmarks? Any distinguishing scars? The questions came as rapidly as volleys of gunfire, like a verbal firing squad.

That was, if it could be called such, the most pleasant part of the process. Everything went downhill from there.

The next step added insult to injury, or maybe vice versa.

Whatever horror stories you've heard about strip searches, they're true. Yes, they make you bend over and cough. I'll leave that right there. You'd think the humiliation of that procedure alone would be enough to prevent repeat offenses. I know I never want to go through it again.

They even wore rubber gloves to go through the pockets of my clothing. I have no idea what they expected to find that would require the protection of rubber gloves. Or was it to keep their own fingerprints off my pocket items? Not that they found anything incriminating.

The strip search was followed by a jailhouse shower. It wasn't all that different from showering at home except for one major and humiliating detail. You're scrubbing your butt-naked self in front of a guard. I'd like to hope that jail personnel consider monitoring inmate showers to be one of their more objectionable duties.

From there I was issued a blue jumpsuit, as opposed to the orange ones made famous by the TV show, and a pair of black flip-flops. Dressed in the local attire, a couple more guards escorted me to the holding cell.

Again, unlike a typical TV-show jail, the cell to which I was conducted had no iron bars. Instead, with the rear and side walls made of concrete, and the front wall of plexiglass from top to bottom, I thought it resembled a cage in a zoo.

Naturally, that prompted a new concern. *What kinds of wild animals are they throwing me in with?*

The cell contained ten or twelve bunkbeds, a single long, metal table, and several drab plastic chairs. It also had a shower in one corner, a drinking fountain, and a toilet that stood in plain view of everybody, including the female guards outside.

When the holding cell's rugged door grated shut behind me, to the accompaniment of ear-numbing deep blasts like an air-horn, the full weight of my situation struck me like a wrecking ball.

I'm in a real mess.

Three or four emotions nailed me all at once. I went from seriously nervous to downright scared to worried about Tonya in less time than it takes to say it. My greatest concern was for Tonya, back in Kentucky. She had no idea what was going on, of course, and I knew she'd be anxious when she couldn't get hold of me, and we were both worried about my daughter's health.

I had a more immediate matter to confront, however. I found myself face-to-face with five or six other men.

At least for the moment. It soon became clear that the holding cell did a good imitation of a revolving door. Guards constantly seemed to be bringing in somebody new or escorting somebody else out. In my rattled state, I wasn't sure how many men actually were there when I first arrived.

"What're you in for?" one of them asked.

That was the standard introductory question, I learned. Not your name, but your alleged crime. I briefly wondered if the length of your rap sheet and the seriousness of the offenses on it determined your place in the jailhouse pecking order.

"Uh, a kilo of coke," I said.

"Serious, man?" said one shadowy figure, and they all drew in a little closer.

I really wanted to take a step back but I could already feel plexiglass pressing my shoulder blades.

"So, what's your story?" asked another.

"Well, the DEA—" I began.

I got no further. The first guy cut me off in mid-sentence. "*Never* say you're working with anybody." His expression grew downright threatening. "You'll be dead before—"

A third guy cut him off in turn, a white guy, blond, probably in his late twenties or early thirties. He stood about five-foot-ten but he was really skinny, and I noticed that he kept to himself, maintaining some distance from the others. "Take this as a very good tip, man," he said, in a friendlier manner than the first guy. "Stop talking. *Now*."

I don't know how long I stood there facing the inmates-of-the-moment before a guard came to the door and said, "Green, you can make your call now."

I wasted no time scooting out that door, and I released a pent-up breath as I stepped through. The guard took me to a standard pay phone in a lobby.

The only phone number I knew that hadn't slipped my memory belonged to Tonya. She was in Kentucky with Tiffany.

I abruptly remembered that I had promised to call her back in a few minutes when we'd ended our earlier call due to that fateful knock on the door.

The door they smashed. It wasn't even locked! If they'd bothered to try the doorknob they could've walked right in.

Was that two hours ago, or three?

I had no idea by then how long ago that had been.

She'll be freaking out by now.

The guard said, "You only have one minute, Green, so you'd better make it quick."

I found that kind of hard to do when I was still in the fog of shock. I punched in Tonya's number and stood there listening to it ring. . . and ring. . . and ring.

Worry clutched my innards. *What's happened to my wife? Why isn't she answering?*

It felt like forever before her voicemail kicked in. By then my guard had begun to slip me warning cues like tapping at his wristwatch with his thick forefinger. "You're down to ten seconds, Green."

Great.

When the tone sounded, I drew myself up. *I've got to be strong for her, got to be a rock. I don't want her to think that I'm not okay and have her hear it in my voice.*

"Tonya," I said as evenly as I could, "I'm in the Utah County Jail. I'm okay, I'm safe, there's no need to worry. Darren's on it and we're working it out. Don't worry about me, I'm okay. Everything will be okay."

By the time the arrest happened, Darren had become more well-to-do than the rest of the family and I knew he had an attorney.

"Time's up, Green," the guard said.

I left Tonya a hurried goodbye and he escorted me back to the common area. I wished that I had had time to tell Tonya about the broken door, and our dogs not being safe, but hoped that she would call our daughter and have her stop by.

I didn't learn Tonya's side of the story until several days later, when she came home from Kentucky.

"I had a huge feeling about what had happened," she told me. "I didn't know for sure, but my gut told me it was something really bad, and I had a sneaky feeling it had to do with Silk Road. I was right.

"I was very relieved to hear your voice. I was so nervous for you. You're not the tough-guy persona, you know. You're too sweet to have survived very long in jail. I was so relieved when you were released quickly."

She was also terrified that she might be arrested. She knew a lot about my work on the Silk Road, and she felt lucky that she'd been out of the house when I was busted, suspecting that if she had been home, she would have been swept up in the net, too.

By the time I returned to the holding area it contained at least ten men.

I learned about my cellmates little by little. The white kid, it turned out, had been sitting in there for two weeks. In Utah somebody has to pick you up when you're released from jail and he didn't have anybody who would come for him.

That's tough, I thought. *When I get out, I'll come back and sign for his release.*

The other inmates peppered me with questions, and I had no qualms about answering. In fact, in my nervousness I began to ramble again. After a few minutes the white kid leveled a glower on me, shook his head in apparent disgust, and wandered off to his corner. He didn't talk to me again after that.

Well, there goes your ride, you jerk.

Looking back at it now, I wonder if he did it to protect me and I feel bad that I didn't go back for him. I suspect that in his own odd way he was trying to warn me that I was still talking too much.

Eventually I began to relax as I learned that my cellmates were all basically nice guys who'd gotten caught in difficult circumstances. Some seemed to have drug or alcohol problems, another appeared to be mentally ill, and others were just young and stupid. Yet they all went in the same cell, as if we had only one answer to a myriad of problems.

One guy had been picked up on his fourth DUI and was awaiting transfer to Salt Lake County.

A big Black man told me, "I was supposed to be released in about a month." He'd been brought in for dealing drugs. "They offered me a choice of probation for two years or ten months in jail. I took the ten months in jail."

"*What?* You've got to be crazy!" I exclaimed.

He shrugged and grinned. "Who wants to be under a lease for two years? In here I've got free meals, free medical, and free rent, and I don't have anything better to do."

I shook my head in disbelief.

A few of my cellmates were Mexicans waiting for ICE officers to deport them back to Mexico.

Time to dust off the Spanish from my mission.

Castellan, the form of Spanish spoken in Spain, is at least as different from the Spanish used in our hemisphere as British English is from the American version. Still, I had kept myself fluent and I knew they would understand most if not all of what I said.

Mostly they needed a little help, I learned when I started chatting with them. They didn't have any soap to take a shower, for one thing, and no one to translate for them.

Being able to assist them distracted me from my own anxieties. I relaxed as I lost myself in my old mission language.

In jail, a new inmate is called a "fish," because they tend to band together, to move in schools. But I didn't feel quite like I fit in, somehow. If I was a fish, I was a loner.

During the afternoon we were allowed to spend time in a common area that had TVs, phones, and more comfortable chairs than the cheap plastic ones in the cell.

While my cellmates settled in to watch whatever was blaring from the TVs, I sought ways to communicate with the outside. Having been unable to reach Tonya with my one allotted call, I fell back on what I'd been told during booking. I spoke to a guard, who took me back to the lobby a couple of different times to call a bondsman.

Sometimes I used the pay phones in the common area. Several bondsmen had their numbers plastered all around the phones.

That's how the system works. Bondsmen are intermediaries. You can call them for free, as many times as you need to and talk for as long as you want. I wondered if some inmates used them simply as listening ears for venting.

I used the service to relay messages to Amanda and Darren, whose phone numbers I'd remembered once the shock diminished and I'd calmed down. The bondsman called them for me, then called back with their replies.

The local police had brought me in shortly after noon and the booking process had taken at least an hour. It became obvious pretty soon that I was going to be there for supper. Not that it mattered to me. I wasn't hungry from missing lunch. I had no desire for food.

The procedure for getting meals felt like a replay of junior high, except the lunchroom staff wore uniforms.

Though the guards wore only radios and maybe mace, no sidearms in the holding area, they still made it plain who was in charge. They spoke in stern, commanding voices, glowered at us as if we were something smelly on the soles of their polished shoes, and leaned in or gestured sharply at us to encourage our compliance.

I noticed that they seemed a little less brusque with the inmates they'd come to know, as if they'd developed some kind of unspoken rapport.

It'd be nice to have them treat me with more courtesy, but I hope I'm not here that long.

They ordered us to form a line and marched us to the kitchen, only about thirty yards from the holding area. There we shuffled along a stainless-steel counter while the kitchen workers placed food on our plastic trays. Then we were paraded back to the cell to eat at that single, long table.

Yeah, junior high except with colorful jumpsuits for school uniforms.

The chicken nuggets were better than I expected but I had too much on my mind to be interested in food. It didn't bother me that the portions were small. Other inmates gaped at me when I pushed my food tray away, still mostly full. I couldn't figure out where I should put it because I didn't see any dirty ones to stack it with. "Where do I put this?" I asked.

"What you doin', man, throwin' away all that food?" someone asked me in astonishment.

"Hey, man, are you gonna eat that?" another guy asked when he noticed I'd barely touched anything. "I'll take it if you're not gonna."

"I'll eat whatever you don't want," someone else begged.

I pushed my tray down the table. "Help yourselves, guys."

"That apple, that's worth a couple cigarettes in trade!" somebody pointed out.

While some inmates used particular foods, especially fruit, as trading commodities, I quickly discovered that most of them literally licked their trays clean to get every crumb.

That explains why I wasn't able to find the stack for dirties when we carried our trays back to the kitchen. There weren't any that appeared to be used.

I suspected that some of the inmates constantly felt hungry. The fact that I gave most of my food to them made me a few friends among my cellmates.

By the time supper was done, I knew I'd be spending the night in jail as well. I slogged into the common area with my cellmates, hoping to forget my anxieties with a little television. Nothing on the tube appealed to me, however. Not anything the other guys wanted to watch, at least.

While I sat there wondering about my fate a young woman, probably in her early twenties, entered the common room. Because it was a males-only area, she stood out like the star on top of a Christmas tree. Young, blonde, petite, and very pretty, she surveyed the room briefly, her fine eyebrows scrunched as if searching for something.

Every head in the room, including mine, wrenched in her direction. Guys' eyes lit up and they straightened in their seats, trying to appear less like prisoners and more like gentlemen, I suppose. I heard a few subdued whistles as she started briskly across the room.

To my amazement, she paused in front of me and asked, "Are you Curtis Green?"

When I said, "Yes, I am," she slipped me a scrap of paper, performed a swift but graceful about-face, and withdrew the way she had come. Every eye watched her leave.

Thoroughly puzzled by her lack of an explanation, I barely heard a couple of guys call, "Wow, Green, how do you rate?" and "What did you do to get a visitor like her?"

I simply unfolded the note. It said,

"Here's Darren's lawyer's phone number. . ."

I learned later that she had come from a lawyer's office. Someone suggested she was my lawyer's daughter, who was a guard there.

Later that evening we were ordered back into the cell. I claimed a bottom bunk, but I found it next to impossible to sleep.

It really wasn't about being confined with six to ten other men of dubious character at any given moment. Nor was it about the noise and lights in the guards' adjoining area, though that certainly didn't help.

There was a *lot* of noise. The klaxon went off every time the guards brought in somebody new or took somebody away, with a blast like the screech of an eighteen-wheeler's air brakes or a freight train's warning horn at a crossing. The guards talked and laughed and the TV blared. Every little noise seemed to reverberate off the concrete walls, so it sounded like a train station or an airport.

To my relief, the place didn't stink of body odor and bodily functions. Instead it oozed an institutional smell that reminded me of the cleaning chemicals used in that training school for the mentally handicapped.

This was in spite of that lone toilet, standing in plain view of everyone in the cellblock. Because even the female guards could see in, my cellmates gathered and stacked all the plastic chairs around it to provide some semblance of privacy whenever they had to go.

The guards switched off some of the lights after the ten o'clock news, but several bright ones still glared into the cell. It was like trying to sleep under a searchlight.

Watching the news was odd, too. They wouldn't let us see the first five minutes or so because that's when they gave the local crime report. I learned from a guard that law enforcement personnel didn't want the inmates to know who they might be bringing in, or what might be happening with their criminal buddies on the outside. It was a form of operations security, I suppose.

None of that affected my ability to sleep as much as my racing heart and all the questions that churned through my mind. Even more than that, I worried about Tonya and my daughters. Not to mention the fact that the ache in my back from being stomped on had worsened. I have four herniated discs, so I'm never pain-free, even on good days.

Unable to get comfortable, I didn't waste a lot of time tossing and turning and shifting on that bunk.

"Hard" was an understatement. It felt like metal plating. I had been issued a pad about an inch thick, an item that would never be mistaken for a real mattress, along with a single lightweight blanket. Both were completely inadequate in that freezing cell. I think I slept for about an hour, at most.

Sleepless but restless, I paced as well as I could among the scattered chairs. My mind ran free. Actually, it ran amok with anxieties.

And me without my Xanax.

I hope Tonya and the girls are all right. I hope they'll be all right. The front door is busted in, so the house is wide open. I hope everything will be okay.

Worry gnawed at me like a rat chewing around the edges of my psyche.

I paused at the drinking fountain in the corner several times, more out of lack of anything better to do and because it was there than from real thirst. Unfortunately, the fountain wasn't exactly quiet. Its handle squeaked, its pump growled the way Max had at the SWAT team, and the water splashed noisily in its basin. After I'd made a few stops, the guys in the closest bunks began to grumble.

"If you turn that thing on one more time, Green," one shadowy shape muttered from a top bunk, "I'm gonna shove your head under the water!"

So I sat on my bunk and stared at my hands, knotted between my knees. *Will this night ever end?*

11: Courts in Cyberspace

Utah County Jail

Thursday, January 17, 2013

Cybertechnology is reshaping our world, from how we work, to how we purchase items on the internet, and to how police work is done, and I suspect that this is just the beginning. A hundred years ago, in nearly every city, the courthouse was the most monolithic structure in town, a monument to our legal system. But in twenty years, with the use of cameras and chatrooms, will the world realize that we no longer need courthouses? And how will the legal system be able to keep imposing its power and influence in the cyber age?

I felt foggy from the lack of sleep by the time the lights came back on at 7:00 the next morning. At least they didn't play a bugle call, or yell and bang on things, but I was still coughing up blood.

They served oatmeal with fruit for breakfast, but I still had no appetite. My mind seemed to be caught in a continuous loop of *How long am I going to be stuck in here? What's going on with Tonya and the girls?* I couldn't do much more than pick at my food so my cellmates started laying dibs on the contents of my tray.

I wasn't allowed to clean up at all before I went before the judge. There was no washbasin in the cell, and I had no comb, no razor, no toothbrush, no deodorant. I smoothed my hair the best I could with my hands but I probably looked like I'd spent the night in a drunk-tank. My back was in constant pain, and I didn't have so much as an Advil for it. It shredded what little human dignity I had left.

Sometime around 9:00 AM a police officer came to the cell door and shouted, "Green!" I rose from the bunk where I'd been sitting and he motioned sharply. "Come with me. You're supposed to appear before the judge now."

Why does this feel like The Green Mile? I couldn't help thinking as the officer marched me through a long, tiled hallway. He hadn't handcuffed me or anything, but my hair still rose on the back of my neck.

The Utah County jail is huge, so I had expected there to be some kind of courtroom. The room to which I was taken, however, had no judge's bench and no witness boxes. Instead, carpeting covered its floor and it contained rows of upholstered pews. It even had the same kind of stand or podium in front that is typical in small LDS chapels.

They probably hold services in here on Sundays, I realized. *I hope I'm not in here long enough for that.*

The major difference from an LDS chapel was its audio-visual equipment, including cameras aimed toward the stand and a large TV facing it.

At the moment, the TV displayed a view of an empty high-backed wooden chair positioned behind the judge's bench, upon which lay a gavel and a sheaf of papers.

This is different. Hearing by video teleconference?

I glanced across the room. Only one other prisoner, a woman, and her guard sat there. Like me, she wore no handcuffs either.

Where are our lawyers? I wondered. *Where's Darren?*

My heart rate bumped up a few notches.

They were at the courthouse eight miles away, it turned out, but I didn't learn that until afterward.

We heard "All rise" through the TV, followed by a scraping and creaking of chairs and a rustling of clothes as people at the distant end stood.

In a few moments the judge swished into view. He seated himself behind the bench with a billow of black robes, picked up the gavel, and banged the pad on the bench's polished top. "This court will now come to order."

The papers I had noticed earlier appeared to contain the details of each person's case. The judge flipped through them briefly, his mouth pursed so he resembled an ancient tortoise, before he peered up at the camera over the rims of his glasses and called a female name.

Her guard motioned the woman forward to the microphone.

The judge's features tightened into sternness, and he leveled steely eyes on her as he read out the charges against her.

Both the prosecutor and her defense attorney were located at the distant courthouse and a discussion ensued. The cameras there must have been placed in several locations because, from my place in the pews, I could see everyone in the courtroom. I searched it for Darren.

What happens if he wasn't able to get hold of his lawyer? Will they set my bail without him?

Partly because of my sore back and partly in an effort to stay awake after my sleepless night, I couldn't sit still. I shifted around to relieve the back pain until my guard shot a warning glower at me.

"Curtis Clark Green," the judge announced as the woman returned to her seat, her face somber.

The court officer beckoned. I stepped up to the microphone, feeling dazed. "Curtis Green, your honor."

He read the charges against me: One count of possession with intent to distribute one kilo of cocaine. I heard the judge's voice as if through thick fog.

Then he set down the paper and fixed his grim gaze directly on me. "Mr. Green, do you understand the charges against you?"

I nodded. "Yes, your honor."

"Very good." He looked away from the camera, off to the side. "Defense?"

A man I'd never seen before rose to his feet. "Your honor," he said, "Attorney Scott E. Williams, defense for Mr. Green."

Mr. Williams proceeded to inform the judge that I had no prior history of involvement with illegal drugs of any kind, that I had lived in Spanish Fork my entire life, and that I was a member of a large and well-respected family in the area. He also emphasized two or three times that I was cooperating fully with the authorities.

That'll go a long way with my bail, I thought, and felt a good deal of relief. My pulse rate, which had quickened at once when the judge called my name, began to relax once more.

The usual discussion between prosecution and defense devolved into a flow of monotonous voices from the TV and my exhaustion settled in once more. I gripped the sides of the podium and fought to keep my eyes open out of fear that I might fall asleep on my feet.

Somewhere at the fringes of my slipping consciousness I heard the remote prosecutor say, "We recommend that bail be set at twenty-five hundred dollars."

Since I'd been told that you usually only pay about a tenth of the set bail, I thought hazily, *Oh good. That's only two hundred fifty dollars.*

I don't know if my attorney misunderstood or if he'd had less sleep than I had because the next thing I heard him say was, "We request a bail of five thousand dollars."

My groggy eyes shot open wide. *What did he say?*

I reached out and fumbled for the microphone. "Your honor," I said, unable to contain my urgency, "I'll take the twenty-five hundred."

I actually came *this close* to parroting a contestant on *Jeopardy* and blurting out, "Alex, I'll take bail-bonds for twenty-five hundred." Chalk it up to sleep deprivation.

I heard abrupt silence for a second or two followed by several chuckles, not only from the viewers at the courthouse but also from the jumpsuit-clad woman sitting behind me. Even the judge's firm mouth momentarily quirked upward in the hint of a smile.

I have a feeling I was the only one who didn't feel amused. My heart rate had stepped up again. *Are they really gonna make it five thousand?* I wiped damp palms on my jumpsuit legs.

After a lot of back-and-forth, they finally set my bail at twenty-five hundred dollars, which turned out to be the lowest amount set for anyone that day.

"I never heard nobody set his own bail before," the woman inmate chortled from the pew behind me when I returned to my place.

I shrugged a response. *All I want to do now is to get out of here.*

That didn't happen for another five interminable hours. I still have no idea why it took so long. My guard steered me back to the holding cell. While I waited, I divided my time between pacing and sitting on my bunk. Time seemed to crawl, the way it does in a nightmare when you're trying to outrun some bogeyman and your feet can't move.

Well, I am in a nightmare. Man, I just want the heck out of here. When am I going to wake up and discover it was all a bad dream?

"Has my brother come yet?" I kept asking the guards.

"We'll tell you when he does," they repeatedly told me.

When they exchanged glances and rolled their eyes after the third or fourth time I realized I must sound like a little kid on a car trip who keeps asking, "Are we there yet?" I'd begun to understand how the kid trapped in the car felt.

Lunch time came and went. I slouched to the kitchen once more with my current cellmates. The "revolving door" of people coming and going had never slowed. Most of my lunch companions this time were different men from the night before.

Chicken nuggets again. There doesn't seem to be much variety to the menu around here. I guess if you're hungry enough though, it doesn't matter what it is as long as you get to eat.

I gave it all away again, mostly to one of the Mexican guys who'd become sort of a friend.

A glance at the large clock in the guards' area showed I'd been in the pokey a full twenty-four hours by the time one of the officers came for me. "Okay, Green, you're out of here," he rumbled.

He escorted me back to the room where I'd changed into the jumpsuit. There he handed me my clothes, sealed in a plastic bag. I tore the bag open and recoiled from the odor.

Unwashed laundry to the third power. Whew!

I can only suppose that sealing my well-worn clothes into the bag had concentrated the smell. At any rate, my nose wrinkled as I pulled them on. The bloodstain from my coughing still blotted the front of my shirt.

Fully clothed but feeling decidedly rumpled and unclean, I followed the officer out to the lobby.

Darren and the bondsman, who was actually a young woman, waited in a small room off to the side. Darren pushed himself up from his chair, his expression melting into one of relief, before he looked me over. "Are you all right, Curtis?"

His relief was nothing compared to how I felt at seeing him. Relief and gladness and gratitude. At that particular moment I totally shut out thoughts of the long hill that I still had to climb.

I also felt deeply embarrassed. I'd never had so much as a traffic ticket in my life, let alone being arrested.

"Yeah," I managed. "I'm pretty stressed out from the whole thing, but I'm okay."

"We were starting to wonder what was going on," Darren said, and indicated the bail woman. "We've been sitting here for five hours. We left the courthouse and came here directly after the hearing."

"*Five hours?*" I stared at him. "I kept asking the guards if you were here yet and they kept telling me 'no.'"

He rolled his eyes. "They knew we were here. Lazy jerks. C'mon, let's get out of here."

We'd barely pulled out onto the highway when Darren slipped me a serious sidelong glance. "You didn't really order cocaine from that Silk Road site, did you?"

I remembered the discussion he and I had before I'd taken the job with DPR, how he'd said he thought it would be all right, and my indignation surfaced beneath my residual tension. "No, of course I didn't order anything! You should know me better than that."

I emphasized, "You're the one who told me you thought it'd be fine to take that job as long as I didn't do any drug dealing myself."

"I did?" He tore his attention from the road ahead to give me a brief stare. "I don't remember telling you that. When did I say so?"

I reminded him of the phone call several months earlier. I quoted parts of it back to him and added that Tonya had been listening as well.

He shook his head, his brow furrowing deeply as it does only when he's angry. "I never told you anything of the kind," he insisted.

I sighed and changed the subject. I told him the whole story of what had happened on the drive home, about Googlyeyed and the N-Bomb, my second thoughts about taking it, and my decision to flush it. I told him about the white van that had parked across the street, the oddly marked box left on my doorstep by the partially uniformed postal inspector, and about the two-dozen human wrecking-balls who had bashed in the front door and ransacked the house.

Darren didn't say much. He just listened. Through his pursed mouth and puckered brow, however, I could read his shock at the whole thing. I just felt immensely grateful that he didn't take the opportunity to lecture me.

"Well, the most important thing to focus on right now," he said with a sigh, "is getting through this and keeping you out of prison."

"Staying out of prison is the most important thing to me," I agreed.

"Some mystery package better not show up at my business now," he added, his face growing grim.

Interestingly, my youngest brother, Marty, later told me that the package of N-bomb had been delivered to Darren's shop a few days before my arrest. Apparently, in one of my many conversations with Googlyeyed, I'd mentioned my brother, and she had confused our addresses.

Marty had no idea what the pills were or where they had come from, so he'd thrown the package out. I can't remember ever being more grateful to see my home than I was when we rolled into the driveway that day. I sagged in the passenger seat for several seconds and stared at it.

The front door still displayed the damaged inflicted by the interagency home-invasion force.

Darren's gaze followed mine. "Looks like they really did a number on it," he remarked.

"Yeah, that'll cost me at least a grand to replace. The door was unlocked. They could've just knocked or walked in."

Darren snorted. "Well, let's go inside."

12: The Shattered House

Spanish Fork, Utah

When a person is arrested, his life is thrown into turmoil. Whether he is guilty or not, he will be shunned by family, perhaps lose his job, and will become a pariah. We punish people for being accused of crimes in our society, not for committing them.

The door to our house had been pulled closed as well as it could be given the amount damage, so it was unlocked when I got home that Saturday morning. I didn't have to try the knob to know that. It had been wrecked badly enough that I wouldn't be able to lock it until I got it repaired.

It would take me a year to replace that door. Had I made a claim within six months, the government would have had to pay for it, but I didn't learn about that until the window of opportunity had closed.

With a glance over my shoulder at Darren, coming up the steps behind me, I pushed the door open.

Max and Sammy's chorus of frantic yapping greeted me before I saw them. They came pelting out of the kitchen, their tiny teeth bared. At first. When they recognized me, they began to leap straight up, over and over. Under other circumstances I would have found it comical. Their excited tail-wagging wiggled their entire little bodies. I gathered both of them up at once and let them lick my face. At least they didn't seem to care about how bad my clothes smelled.

The first thing I noticed in the living room was that the incriminating package, wrapped in its layers of sticky tape, no longer lay on the carpet. No doubt somebody in that official home-invasion force had collected it into an evidence bag. Even the spew of white powder across the carpet had disappeared. Someone had vacuumed.

The SWAT goons wouldn't have done that.

"Amanda?" I called.

No answer.

I didn't have to venture very far through the house to know that my oldest daughter had been there. I hadn't actually seen what kind of damage the break-and-enter team had inflicted, but the noise that had reached me while I lay on the floor and then sat under guard on the couch had warned of much greater destruction than I found as I made my way from room to room.

"I need to take off," Darren said at last. He hadn't come any farther than the front door and he stood with his hand on the loose doorknob. "Will you be okay here by yourself?"

"Yeah, I'll be fine," I assured him. "I need to take a shower and get out of these stinking clothes."

"All right," Darren said. "Call me if you need anything."

He left. I heard him outside for a couple of minutes, trying to wrench the door shut in the broken jamb before his crisp footfalls withdrew to his car.

A glance at the clock in the kitchen, one of the few items left undamaged in the house, read three o'clock.

First things first.

A shower and change of clothes did little to lift my mood.

I soaked my stinking shirt in cold water to try to get out the bloodstains and wondered if I should throw it away.

I spotted my cellphone lying on the kitchen counter when I returned from our bedroom after showering. I have no idea who had placed it there. The last time I remembered seeing it was in the hand of DEA Agent Carl Force.

Nob.

"Call me the second you get out," he'd said.

I paced through the house, phone in hand, making mental notes of all the damage.

My laptop had been taken, the one on which Carl Force had made me communicate with Googlyeyed. The one I had used to do my administrative work on Silk Road.

Oh my gosh, I even gave him my user password! I didn't have to do that. In England if you don't give a user password they can sentence you, but not here in the States. They didn't even make me, I just gave it to them.

I shouldn't have done that. I should've said. . . I should've just said no.

I never did get that computer back. It just "disappeared." I thought for a while that the cops had taken it as evidence, but it disappeared so completely that it could have folded itself up and disappeared into cyberspace.

They had left my personal computer and my bitcoin mining equipment, at least. I found no consolation, no relief in that. I didn't go online at all. I didn't dare.

I wandered around for a while, I don't know how long, doing a little more cleaning up here and there. And I paced, back and forth between the kitchen and living room. That's what I do when I'm stressed. That's why I had done it in the cell.

I started questioning myself, reflecting on what I had done to get myself into such a situation. Why hadn't I gone with my first instincts about the Silk Road site? Why had I taken the stupid job that DPR offered? Why had I even touched that strange package on my doorstep?

Anger with myself knotted my fists and clenched my teeth.

I can't believe how stupid I was! I'm not really like this!

Then I thought of what my family, my siblings, would think. Except for Darren—and even he had seemed to doubt my answer—they would believe I was a drug dealer. When the police label you as a suspect, it's as if it casts a glamour over everyone who sees you.

I knew the story must be all over the local news by now: Curtis Green caught with a kilo of cocaine in his hands.

No one had any idea of the circumstances behind it. No one knew the whole story. I'd been set up, framed by the very same cop who'd arrested me, but that wasn't how anyone following the news would hear it. It would be my word against his.

As I assessed the extent of the damage to the house—the overturned drawers, the battered doors—it struck me that my home was the least of my problems. My personal life and reputation had been wrecked far more badly.

The wrecking wasn't done yet, either. I faced a very real possibility of going to prison for a very long time.

That wouldn't affect only me. It would impact my entire family: my father and my siblings, Tonya and our daughters.

They would be branded with the stigma of having a family member in prison.

For Tonya and the girls there would be the psychological trauma of the house having been raided and ransacked. They would suffer financially without my income.

Feeling overwhelmed, and physically weak from the pain in my back, the continued bleeding from my lungs, and how little I'd eaten or slept in the last twenty-four hours, I returned to our bedroom and flung myself down on the bed, eager to give my back some relief.

As it had during the previous night in the cell, my mind churned with fragmented thoughts.

I've let my family down. My whole family. I don't even care about me anymore. I was raised to be better than this. I'm supposed to be a good little Mormon boy.

How did I get to this point? I don't abuse drugs. I've never used illegal ones. I try to live my life the best I can. Yeah, I've made some stupid mistakes before now. Did it come from greed or what? I don't know, but I know this time I've made a really big mistake.

The magnitude of it unloaded on me like an avalanche. I felt crushed under its weight.

Under that ferocious pressure I could no longer contain the emotions. Dread, grief, self-accusation, and mind-numbing fear all wrestled in my soul. Worst of all, however, was the despair, like a pit into which I'd fallen so deeply that I could no longer see a light at the top.

I wanted to sob.

What have I done, to them as well as to myself? How much are they going to go through now because of me? I've become a burden to all of them. They're better off without me.

I can't. . . leave without telling them goodbye and how much I love them. My love for them is why I have to do this.

I peeled myself off the bed with great effort. With tears still streaking my face, I stumbled back to the kitchen and rummaged through drawers for paper and a pen.

Any pen but that stupid pink one.

Seated at the table, I stared for a long while at that blank sheet of paper.

How do I say this?

My fingers sweated around the pen at first, then cramped.

How do I explain this to them?

I swept tears off my face the whole time. They may have blotched on the paper but I didn't notice. I do know that my hand shook. I could barely keep the pen pressed to the paper.

I spent most of the letter apologizing for the embarrassment this would cause them. "It's not your fault," I emphasized. "I got into this myself. I should have known better."

I offered them advice. "Always go to church. Don't make the mistakes that I've made. Always do what's right. If you're thinking about doing something and you're not sure if it's right, talk to somebody about it. Always make sure you follow the golden rule."

I read it through when I finished it at last, and left it on the table while I surveyed the kitchen.

Where's the best place to put it? They need to find the letter before they. . . see my body.

During my years as an EMT I'd been called to some suicides. Always, always I had wondered how someone could possibly take his own life. I couldn't understand it, couldn't grasp how somebody could get to that low of a point. I just didn't get it.

I do get it now.

I ended up posting the note on the refrigerator with one of the many magnets stuck there.

I'll do it with a knife, I decided.

From that EMT work I knew what kind of damage one could do with a blade. It didn't even have to be very long, just sharp enough to open a large blood vessel.

I'll bleed out quickly. That's practically painless.

I chose one of Tonya's kitchen knives, about five inches long, with a serrated edge. I fingered the blade, testing its sharpness. My hands began to shake again as I entered the family room.

All that blood. Most people don't realize how much blood there is in the human body until they see a pool of it.

I had seen that, more than once.

What will that do to Tonya and the girls, seeing all that blood? How will it affect them?

I knew how it had affected me. I'd had nightmares, even flashbacks of some crash scenes for weeks afterward.

I can't do that to them.

I put away the knife and wheeled back toward the bedroom, wiping fresh tears off my face. I hadn't cried like this since I was a little kid.

I kept a couple of handguns in a safe in the bedroom, guns I had completely forgotten to mention during the goons' Q and A session the day before.

If one of them is still in there...

They were, including my .32. I'd bought it a few years earlier for recreational shooting with my in-laws. Sometimes we'd gone to gun ranges, sometimes out to the country. I hadn't used it in quite a while.

How could the SWAT guys not have found them? I couldn't help wondering. *That safe door was wide open.*

I'll never figure out how they didn't see it. Maybe it's because sometimes the things that are in plain sight are hardest to see.

I loaded the .32 with my hands shaking as violently as they had before, so I could barely accomplish the task. Then I stood there, staring up the barrel. Those two or three minutes felt like an eternity.

One squeeze of the trigger and it'll all be over.

I'd seen splattered brains and smelled the reek of it as an EMT, too.

Over for me, but what about for them?

For the survivors in a suicide, cleaning up is an ordeal. I'd seen brains splattered in bedrooms, or against the side of a house. Clean-up can take hours, and yet the survivors often discover little pieces of the past, like confetti, glued to the wall months later.

At last I hurled the pistol across the room. It bounced off the wall, marring the paint, and struck the carpet with a dull thud.

I left the handgun where it had fallen, half afraid to pick it up even long enough to return it to the safe. Instead, with Max and Sammy at my heels, and mopping away a fresh wave of emotion with a hand that still trembled, I pushed my way back to the living room and collapsed to my knees beside the couch.

Max and Sammy, prancing about on the couch cushions, licked the tears off my face as I began to pray.

As I prayed for long minutes, I finally saw an image of my grandmother, all in white, as if sitting on the bed beside me. She said as if to a child, "Now, now, Curtis, it will be okay."

I don't remember how long I stayed on my knees. I only know that they ached, and I winced when I finally struggled to my feet. But the turmoil in my soul had calmed.

Suicide isn't the answer. It'll be okay. Everything will work out. It may take a while, but it'll all work out.

I released a deep breath of relief and returned to the bedroom for my phone.

I guess I'd better call Carl.

Next question, how do I find his number?

The only number I had belonged to a local postal inspector. Not the guy in shorts who'd interrogated me the day before.

"I'm trying to find a number for a DEA agent, Carl Force," I said.

The local postal guy proved to be helpful. As I began to tap in the number he gave me, Carl's name popped up on my cell.

He could've at least told me that he'd entered it in my phone.

I think it rang twice before an unmistakable, crisp voice said, "Carl Force."

I wanted to snarl, "Hello, Nob." In fact, I wanted to snarl a lot of things at him. But I said, "It's Curtis Green. I'm home. You said to call when I got released?"

"Ah, yes, Curtis," Carl said. "We need to talk. We've got to deal with your mugshot. At this point anybody who would recognize your mugshot is in the—"

I told him about it.

"Yeah, we're working on it," he said. "I've got a call in to somebody who can take it off the websites."

"You'd better do it fast," I said, "or DPR's going to find out I got arrested. That's a major concern to me."

"Yeah, I know, I know, Curtis," Carl said, a bit impatiently. I heard silence from the other end for a few seconds. "So... Monday is a holiday, Martin Luther King Day. Nobody at the jail will be in on Monday, so they can't do anything until Tuesday. Nothing is going to get posted before then."

That did nothing to relieve my anxieties. "Carl, as soon as he finds out," I emphasized, "it's all over. It's all over!"

"Calm down, Curtis, I'm on it," Carl said. "In the meantime, we need to get you back on the Silk Road site. You've been kicked off, you know. We've got to fix this quick. You could be very valuable to bringing DPR down."

In his next breath he said, "You've got to cook up some ideas, a story for why you've been offline, because DPR's been wondering where you've been for the last twenty-four hours."

I considered that. I liked DPR. I hadn't gotten into this because I wanted to bring him down, but a surety crept over me: with my arrest, DPR would have to do something to cover his trail, and I didn't know exactly how far he might go.

Hit men advertise their services on Silk Road.

I mulled that over for several seconds. "Let's see... Well, my wife is out in Kentucky with one of our daughters right now.... She had a medical emergency and she's in the hospital. What if I tell him that?... Yeah, I'll tell DPR that we had to fly out on short notice because of our daughter's medical situation."

"That sounds good," Carl said. I could almost see him nodding. "That gives you an actual excuse to be gone."

Carl told me that the DEA was currently examining the laptop he had taken. I think he called it 'exploiting.' They were, of course, giving special attention to anything related to Silk Road.

DPR had been leaving me messages, Carl continued. Things to the effect of, "Why aren't you clearing out your accounts?" and "Get back to me ASAP!" In his increasing impatience, DPR had finally changed my password and locked me out.

"I wasn't kidding yesterday when I told you it wasn't a good idea to arrest me," I told him.

I heard a chuckle from the other end, which made me grit my teeth. *You jerk! You have no idea what you've done to my life.*

"Calm down, Curtis," Agent Force said. "We'll get it worked out. Here's what we need you to do. . . ."

He promised that if I helped them catch DPR, he'd make sure that the police were lenient with me, that I'd only get probation. There was a thing called "Witness Protection," after all. But they wanted me to go back to work, undercover this time.

Force and his thugs had taken only my main computer. It took me a while to access TorChat with one of my two computers the SWAT guys had left behind. Feeling some trepidation as I recalled DPR's rants for being one minute late, or even early, to online meetings, I composed a message.

What is he gonna say when I've been off for a day and a half now?

I mentally braced myself for the text version of a tongue-lashing.

"I'm sorry that I've been away," I typed. "My daughter in Kentucky had a medical emergency and was taken to the hospital, and my wife and I had to fly out to help her."

The silence from the other end seemed interminable, though it probably only lasted a few minutes. I stiffened when a reply appeared in the queue.

I believe now, in hindsight, that DPR already knew that I'd been arrested, that he was agonizing over what he would have to do.

"Flush, man, it's about damn time!" DPR wrote. "You just can't do that kind of thing, you know? Some of my customers having been waiting more than forty-eight hours for resolutions. I promised them less than twenty-four hours. You can't just take off and leave them hanging like that, understand? You've got to let me know when things come up."

"I'm sorry," I repeated. "It was an emergency. We had to leave right away."

Another sulky interval followed. He didn't say so, but I knew he was worried that I had been compromised.

He didn't even ask how my daughter is doing. That's not like him. But with DPR you never know.

At last another message arrived. "Well, all right. I'll reset your password and let you back on this time. But next time you better let me know first."

"I will," I typed. "Thank you."

I blew out a breath of relief.

DPR never mentioned law enforcement. He never asked if I'd been arrested. Nothing. Nothing! He clearly bought it. I think he's clueless. At least for now.

Carl saw that I was back on Silk Road. He discovered it when DPR reset my old password and Carl couldn't log in. I felt a perverse sense of satisfaction about that.

Emotionally and physically drained as I was, however, I waited until the next morning to get back on Silk Road. Sure enough, my admin inbox contained several thousand requests.

I went to work, then stopped and thought: *But there's something else I need to do first.*

13: Getting Squeezed

Wednesday, January 23, 2013

Spanish Fork, Utah

I've always loved the phrase, "When life gives you a lemon, make lemonade." That's great unless you're the lemon.

Tonya went with me on the fifty-mile drive to Salt Lake. It was just eight days since I'd been arrested. Having her with me in the car eased some of my tension but not all. There had been a lot more silence than usual between us since she'd come home. The uncomfortable kind of silence that feels like low, brooding storm clouds.

We found a dozen or so people from various agencies waiting for us in a conference room at the Secret Service building when we arrived, at about 9:00 in the morning. Carl milled among them, accompanied by an agent he introduced as Shaun Bridges.

Bridges is a little man, with rather large ears that complete a mousy impression. Certainly not the image one would expect for a Secret Service Agent.

"I thought the Secret Service just protects the President," I said.

"We do," Bridges replied. "I've served on some high-profile presidential details. But we also get involved in anything to do with money and the Treasury, and there's a *lot* of money involved in the Silk Road case."

I learned that he had once been in charge of details guarding Michelle Obama, and that raised my opinion of him.

Carl also introduced me to a youthful but aggressive and cocky attorney. "Justin Herring," Carl said. "He's the AUSA, Assistant United States Attorney, and he's in charge today."

We exchanged a quick, curt handshake. "My lawyer mentioned your name to me," I said.

When Tonya started to follow me into the conference room, Carl raised a hand in a 'stop' gesture, like a traffic cop. "I'm sorry, but you can't come in, ma'am."

"Fine," she replied with a bit of a snap. "I'll be down in the lobby. I brought plenty to read." She waved her Kindle in his face and hefted the bag full of books on her arm.

Momentary panic twisted my insides as she pivoted and strode up the tiled hallway, but Carl nudged my shoulder. "Come on, Curtis, let's get this show on the road."

Another brief panic swept over me when I saw how many people actually occupied the conference room. Fifteen at least, maybe eighteen. All people I'd never seen before.

They probably chartered an FBI airplane or something to bring in a crowd like that.

I craned around for a moment and spotted my lawyer among the muttering government personnel, who all milled around with their Styrofoam cups of early-morning coffee. Upon realizing that I had entered, she crossed to me at once.

"We've developed the proffer agreement for you, Curtis," she told me in hushed tones, as if to prevent the others moving through the room from overhearing him. "Basically, what this means for you is that as long as you are completely truthful with the investigators, nothing you say during this session can be used or brought against you, either in prosecution or in sentencing. Do you understand that?"

"Yes, ma'm," I assured her.

"Very good." She nodded stiffly. "On the other hand, if you are untruthful on *any* point and they later discover it, they can tear up this proffer letter and charge you with anything they want. Do you understand that, too?"

A chill tickled my spine at the thought. "Absolutely, sir." The words came out in a stammer.

My attorney nodded once more, and she told me, "It's to your advantage to be completely open and give them as much information as you can."

"I definitely will," I said.

The government's multi-agency debriefing team included a number of computer technicians, who had set up the computer Force had taken in the raid on my home. My laptop now stood open on the conference room's long, generic table. The presence of so many people pressing around and among each other gave the room the impression of being cramped.

Justin Herring motioned me to a swiveling chair at the head of the table. "As a Silk Road administrator, you must have access to the back end of the site."

"Yes, I do," I affirmed.

"What we need you to do," Justin said, "is show us exactly what you do as an administrator on Silk Road. Show us everything, the whole nine yards."

Just as the SWAT team had closed around my kitchen table the previous week, the government personnel gathered behind my chair at the table. I couldn't even see the door. That sent a wave of claustrophobia over me.

I had barely set my butt in the chair before they began to pelt me with questions.

"When did you start getting on Silk Road?" someone asked.

"Do you have any other accounts on the site besides Flush?" asked another, who stood directly behind me.

"I have several," I said. "I opened new ones because I kept forgetting the passwords."

"We need you to tell us what they are," the guy said.

I rattled off all the accounts I could remember. I think I had opened about half a dozen.

"I had Chronicpain to start with," I explained. "I used that on Silk Road while I was moderating the Health and Wellness forum. And there were a couple of others. Got Milk was one."

In my nervousness, I slipped into ramble mode. "I let another guy use Chronicpain for a while. I actually told him to get off, and I used Got Milk at the end of twenty-eleven or beginning of twenty-twelve. He was selling a few illegal things, and I told him, don't sell anything illegal, and he agreed. At least the last time I saw his site, what he was selling, ninety-nine percent of it was legitimate. And the stuff that wasn't legal here *was* legitimate and totally legal in eighty percent of other countries...."

I told them everything that came to my mind, scared that I might omit something that would come back to bite me later.

We spent the next few hours with me walking my debriefers through the whole process. I showed them how I accessed the site, how I resolved disputes and reset passwords for customers, and how to navigate the vendors' pages.

There were some links on the site that I still didn't know what they did. "I have no idea what this thing does," I told them. "I have no idea about this, either. This I do know, and this I know, but this one, I have no idea where it goes."

"Can you pull up any of the website communications?" somebody asked.

"I could," I said, "but it would look funny for me to be in there. I don't know if DPR can see what I'm doing, so I don't want to do anything that's not normally my job."

"Got it," my questioner said. "So DPR still thinks you're managing his admin chores."

"Right." I nodded. "I don't want to raise any flags, so if you ask me to do something I wouldn't normally do, I'm not going to do it."

The bunch of them nodded and murmured agreement.

"You don't want to tip him off that we're on to him," one of them said.

"Exactly," I agreed. "You see, DPR gave me a special entrance to Silk Road through Tor." I swept a glance across my audience of suits. "I don't know if you know how Tor works. You have to go through three different computers. DPR actually has a personal, private Tor bridge."

Eyes widened around the circle, and several people traded elated expressions that might as well have been shouts of "Pay dirt!"

So, I told them about it. I told them in detail and I showed them where it was. "Here it is, right here, and here are the numbers you use to get in."

A handful of taut faces revealed hunger almost to the point of lust to try it right then.

AUSA Herring waved them off. "We'll focus on that tomorrow. We've got other things we need to concentrate on today."

I showed them how bitcoins were used for payment, and how to transfer the bitcoins once customers confirmed that they had received their purchases.

The mousy Secret Service guy, Shaun Bridges, seemed particularly fascinated with that. "Can you show us again how that's done?" he requested.

I showed them, and then Carl Force told Shaun, "Weren't you supposed to be somewhere else today?"

Shaun glanced up at him as if in surprise and said, "Oh, right," and then scurried away, and we went back to work.

Sometime about noon my lawyer grew restless. "I need to get out of here," she said. "I have other things I need to accomplish today. I believe you can handle the rest of this on your own, Curtis." And she left.

I scanned the circle of people leaning in close behind me. "Are we about finished?" I asked.

"Actually, we're just getting started," one of them said. I don't know which agency he belonged to.

The interrogation became grueling. They never broke for lunch. Or supper. My back began to ache from sitting all day. In fact, they didn't call it quits until well after 10:00 that night. By then I felt as if I'd wrung every byte of data out of the Silk Road site that I possibly could.

My body felt as if I'd had every molecule wrung out, too.

I started to breathe a sigh of relief when Justin Herring finally said, "That's enough for tonight." He glanced at me. "We'll let you go home now, Curtis, but we'll need you at the Marriott City Center by eight o'clock tomorrow morning. This being a government facility, it's closed on weekends, so we can't come back here tomorrow."

"Besides," Carl said, "the Marriott's conference room is larger and a lot more comfortable."

I stared from one to the other. "It's an hour and a half drive each way, and I'm wiped out. I'll never make it back to Salt Lake by eight tomorrow morning."

"Get a hotel room around here, then," somebody said.

"With what?" I shot back. I didn't have any cash, nothing left at all. I said hopefully, "If you guys can give me the money to pay for it, I will."

Several of the government guys exchanged glances. One even rolled his eyes. But Carl said, with mild resignation, "Let's see if we can get Curtis and his wife a room where we're staying. That'll be easier for everybody."

To my complete surprise, all the agents started pulling bills, tens and twenties, out of their wallets and handing them to me.

Late though it was on a Friday night, someone got on his cell and learned there were still a few rooms left at the Fairfield Inn.

Tonya lifted her attention from her book when I entered the lobby. She tucked it into her bag and stood, her eyes searching my face and clearly wondering if it was finally over.

"They're putting us up in the Fairfield for the night," I told her. "They want me back at the Marriott City Center first thing in the morning."

"*What?*" Her tone bore incredulity. "They've had you up there for thirteen hours and they're not done with this *yet?*" In the next heartbeat, however, she slipped into planning mode. "If we're staying overnight, I need to get contact solution and a few other things." She shook her head and glowered at the backs of the personnel already exiting the building.

Outside, a fog settled that was so dense, I could hardly see my hand in front of my face. My eyes felt bleary from fatigue, so Tonya drove us, following the taillights of the agents in front of us, just so that we could find our way.

She dropped me off at the Fairfield Inn, a car or two after Carl, and took off to run errands. I found Carl hanging around the front desk when I came in.

"We need a room for Mr. Green and his wife for one night," he informed the desk clerk.

"Thanks," I said, and handed the clerk the handful of bills. He slapped a key card into my hand.

Carl favored me with a brief, tight smile. "Breakfast is at seven, Curtis. They've got a nice buffet here. Get some sleep."

In my exhaustion, I stumbled along the carpeted corridor to the room. If anyone had seen me, they probably would've thought I'd been partying a little too hard. It took a couple of tries with the key card to make the lock's light blink green.

The first thing I spotted on pushing the door open was the king-sized bed. I crossed to it in a couple of strides, and barely heard the door clunk shut behind me as I fell flat down on top of it on my face. I didn't even take off my shoes, let alone my shirt, or bother with turning down the covers. I simply flopped across it with my feet hanging over the side.

I don't have any idea when Tonya came in. I roused enough at that point to get into the bed properly.

I didn't fall back to sleep for some time, however, after Tonya slid in beside me. My eyes fixed on the ceiling, where a slender shaft of light from outside, shooting through a narrow gap between the curtains, highlighted its texture. My nerves had kicked in, spurred by one thought that kept racing through my mind.

I'm going to prison. I know it. That proffer agreement won't keep me out even if I do tell these guys one hundred percent of the truth.

Another thought kicked in as well.

They were the ones who suggested getting us a room here, not me. They probably put us up here to keep an eye on me. I'm sure of it.

14: More Frames than an Art Gallery

Marriott City Center, Salt Lake City, Utah

Saturday, January 26, 2013

The propensity for humans to be cunning and evil should never surprise you.

Eventually, too worn out to keep worrying, I sank into sleep once more. I slept deeply, and woke with a groan when the wake-up call came.

That was good, but I sure could've used a few more hours.

Probably due to the lack of meals the day before, I found I had a huge appetite for breakfast. The aromas of bacon and rolls and fresh coffee that reached us as Tonya and I emerged from the elevator on the ground floor were enough to prompt a rumble from my stomach and get my mouth watering.

We found several members of the government team already in the breakfast room when we entered.

"Mr. and Mrs. Green, why don't you come join us?" called Sherry, one of the few female agents in the mix. She waved us toward her table, which she shared with a short, skinny, dark-haired guy with thick facial hair. He was in his late thirties or early forties, I estimated.

Both Sherry and her dark-haired cohort were from Homeland Security in Baltimore. She engaged us in light conversation while we ate, but he remained quietly focused on his food.

As Carl had mentioned the previous evening, Fairfield Inn did have a very good breakfast buffet, complete with one of those make-your-own-waffle machines. I took full advantage of the offerings, spurred on by the previous day's involuntary fast.

Blonde, attractive, and about the same age as her HLS counterpart, Sherry told us over breakfast, "I know this must be extremely difficult for both of you, but we're very grateful for your help. We appreciate your willingness to come forward with so much information. With your assistance, we're figuring out what's going on. I think everything is going well."

"Do you have any idea how long it's going to go on today?" Tonya asked.

"You should probably expect another full day," Sherry's dark-haired fellow agent answered. That was about the only thing he said through the whole meal.

Tonya sighed. "I'm going to go home then, Curtis. It doesn't do any good for me to be here if they won't let me into the room. I'll take you to the City Center on my way out of town. Give me a call when it looks like you're starting to wind down and I'll come back."

"No need for that, Mrs. Green," Sherry said. "We can give him a ride home."

I worried briefly. I knew that Tonya was afraid of me getting arrested, but the ride home would be greatly appreciated.

I felt refreshed after the good breakfast, and a bit more optimistic as we left the Fairfield, despite secretly wishing that Tonya would stay. But I knew it really would be a waste of her time.

As I entered the Marriott City Center, I glanced around the spacious, elegant lobby with its cream-colored ceiling and floor and its wood-paneled walls. Carl hovered near the front desk, obviously waiting for me. "Doing okay, Curtis?"

"I got some good sleep," I replied, "but I really could've used a few more hours."

"Well, you may get a chance for that," Carl said. He gestured toward a nearby grouping of sofas. "Make yourself comfortable. They're not ready for us upstairs yet."

We were still sitting there at 9:00, and Tonya gave a sigh and rose. "I need to get going, Curtis. I'll see you tonight."

I sat for another hour and a half or two hours. I'm not sure which. Eventually, the hours of sleep I hadn't gotten caught up with me. My head drooped to my chest, and I sagged in the comfortable chair.

A hand on my shoulder shook me awake. I started and stared up into the face of a smartly uniformed employee.

"Sir," he said, his expression firm, "I'm sorry but I have to ask you to leave the premises."

Before I'd fully roused from my grogginess, I glimpsed Carl and a couple of the other government agents bee-lining in my direction from wherever they'd been pacing.

"It's all right," Carl told the employee. "He's part of our group. We're just waiting for the room to be set up."

The young man appeared dubious, but after a few seconds' hesitation he slipped away.

I watched him go. *Did he think I was a bum, coming in to catch a few minutes of warmth from the cold?*

I guess I looked worse than I'd imagined.

When he'd gone and the other agents spread out again, Carl crouched by my chair and put a hand on my shoulder. "Things got a little more complicated overnight," he confided. "We found a message from DPR. He's accusing you of stealing a million in bitcoins."

I gaped at him, in complete shock. "A *million* in bitcoins? There's—you've got to be kidding me!"

"No, I'm not." He shook his head, his face serious. "He says you stole a million *dollars' worth* of bitcoins."

At the current exchange rate, I knew, it took about 350 thousand bitcoins to equal one million dollars. I wondered if someone really had stolen them? It wouldn't have been DPR. He wasn't about money. I was so deep in shock, I could hardly think.

"So, the others did a little searching," Carl went on, "and dug up some evidence that you were looking at how to get a passport. They think you were planning to flee the country."

I couldn't stop staring at him. "That was one of my daughters, about six months ago. Is my attorney here?"

I really felt I needed her badly. I wondered if my proffer agreement had gone out the window, after I'd given them the keys to the kingdom.

"Haven't seen her," Carl said.

I fumed. But I certainly had no more desire to sleep after that. In fact, the jitters began to set in.

We finally went upstairs around 11:00. We didn't take the elevator very far, maybe only to the third floor.

We emerged into a broad hallway with plush, Oriental-style, red carpet and large, circular chandeliers glittering above small, round, black tables bearing flower arrangements.

"We've got a suite for the day," Carl said. "Several more people have arrived for this session."

"More people? From where?" I wondered.

They'd gotten a *big* suite, one of the largest in the hotel, I think. It seemed to just keep going. As I gazed across the first room, I kept seeing other rooms beyond it.

A really nice suite, of course, I thought. They're spending the government's money.

The front room was comprised of a little foyer. Then I saw a little computer area with a desk. If you went to the right, there was the bathroom, and then beyond it the bedroom. It was a pretty big area back there, with large windows. A couch stood on that side, and I saw couches in the bedroom as well.

I wonder how much of my tax money goes to pay for things like this?

At least twenty-five people appeared to be squeezed into the suite, spacious though it was. They spoke in subdued but hurried voices between slurping from their coffee cups.

"Most of the new folks are with a company we've brought in to do the computer hacking," Carl explained. "They're a private company, a subcontractor."

If he mentioned the company's name I didn't catch it. I simply nodded and surveyed the newcomers. I learned later that sometimes the government uses foreign intelligence agencies to gather information that might be otherwise illegal for them to obtain, but I can't be sure that this is what they were up to.

The two who stood out most were tall, blond, and probably in the same age-range as Sherry and her short, dark-haired, HLS counterpart, but they weren't conversing in English. I caught snatches of some heavy, guttural accent.

Swedish? East European? I bet it's either German or Swedish.

The computer technicians I'd seen the day before had set up my laptop on a big table that had been brought into the suite's outer room.

Justin Herring rushed toward me as I stood surveying the activity from the doorway. "Good, you're here," he said. "We're getting a late start today, so we need to get going." He pointed me toward the chair in front of my laptop.

I sat down and, at the fringes of my vision, saw the small crowd of dark suits settle like a murder of crows wherever they could find a place to perch with a good view of what I was doing. The sofa, every chair, even the top of the suite's nearby desk. They weren't packed quite as tightly as they'd been in the Secret Service office the day before, but it was still enough to make me nervous.

Déjà vu all over again.

"Okay, you can go ahead and log in now," somebody said.

My hands always shake when I'm nervous. I unclenched them from each other in my lap and set them on the keyboard. My quivering fingers were all over the place as I typed in my password and username.

It didn't work.

I tried again: password, username.

No joy.

I think I tried it six times. With the pressure of a couple dozen pairs of eyes riveted on my every move, my hands' shaking only increased. Especially when nobody said a word. The silence made it even worse.

Not to mention the pounding echoes of Carl's warning earlier. "DPR is accusing you of stealing a million in bitcoins."

How many people in this room know about that?

Probably all of them. And not being able to get in screams "Guilty!" Like I'm messing up the passwords on purpose to keep them out.

That never-mentioned matter loomed like a ghost over the room. My hands began to sweat as well as to shake. But anger rippled through my anxiety, too.

All of them know what the username and password are. I told them as soon as DPR gave me the new one.

Finally, one of the guys rose from his place on the arm of the sofa. "Here, let me do it. Your hands are shaking too hard."

I shoved myself out of the chair and let him sit down.

Like me, the other guy tried it five or six times.

I watched him with my teeth clenched.

It's not working. Maybe somebody really did hack in. When people do that, they'd have to take away their victims' account access and change the password so the victim's account will send the money to them.

While the young man labored away, making every keystroke with deliberate exactness, another of the computer guys began to barrage me with questions.

"Mr. Green, do you know how to hack into a computer?" he asked. "Do you know how to program?"

I snorted. "I know how to change HTML to bold, maybe," I said, "or to a new color. Just simple, basic, grade-school type stuff like that. But that's all."

As if he hadn't heard me, he repeated his questions. Did I know how to hack? Did I know anything about programming?

He asked me the same questions over and over, over and over, over and over, but each time with a slightly different choice of words.

Does he think I don't understand what he's asking?

Exasperated, I finally snapped. "Look, dude, how many times do I have to tell you I *don't know* how to hack! I'm *not* a programmer. I don't know anything about it."

Isn't that supposed to be your job? I thought.

Looking back on it, I think they knew, regarding the stolen money Carl had told me about, that it would've taken a skilled hacker to do it. Of course, they thought that hacker was me.

Now, at this time, Silk Road was always getting hacked. Always. I'd seen it even before I started moderating the health-and-wellness forum. People went in and changed pictures on the vendor sites and stole money constantly.

"Dude," I said, "Silk Road gets broken into all the time. This doesn't surprise me a bit."

And it didn't. I just hadn't imagined that someone would hack into *my* account.

Justin Herring finally waved a hand to get the room's attention. "We need to concentrate on that Tor bridge today," he said. "Mr. Green, why don't you show us how it works?"

The hungry light I'd seen in several faces the day before returned as if somebody had flipped a switch. Eager eyes shifted toward me, and some people leaned forward in their seats.

This is the Holy Grail, and they know it.

"A Tor bridge stays on your computer," I told the little crowd. "You have to go to a special place to access it, but it's always there. DPR can't take it off my computer." I patted my laptop before I put my hands on the keyboard once more. "He could disable it, but—"

Apparently DPR *had* disabled it. I couldn't get into Tor.

I can't access Silk Road. I can't get into Tor.

I puffed out a breath and addressed the huddled agents. "It looks like he's disabled that bridge. But it doesn't matter. Once you have that Tor, that node, you have access to the first computer, and that doesn't take much. You've already been given access. There are three steps."

I proceeded to give my audience the first step, the Tor address.

"I've got you through the first wall now," I said, and indicated my monitor, "but you have to go through two more. You can do that with some serious computer work, but if you don't have that first step there's no way you can get in. Just your password doesn't work."

Heads bobbed in comprehension all around the room. Fingers tapped notes into various handheld devices.

I glanced up at Carl once when I paused. He stood leaning against the wall, his muscled arms crossed over his chest, his eyes narrowed on some undetermined point, and his mouth pursed. He didn't seem to be following my presentation at all.

He's thinking about DPR's accusation that I stole all that money.

A chilly prickle crept over my scalp.

I proceeded to demonstrate how to use the Tor bridge well into the afternoon, answering the questions of the computer technicians and agents from the various organizations.

We paused for lunch only when somebody who had slipped out returned with a couple of large bags of Subway sandwiches. It had been a long time since breakfast, but I was barely aware of eating my sandwich, focused as I was on demonstrating the Tor bridge and answering everybody's questions.

When I wrapped it up at about 9:00 that night, the crowd thinned quite a bit. All the computer technicians thanked me for the detailed information, and the big European guys shook my hand. Everyone one of them wore smiles like cats who'd just eaten the family goldfish for lunch.

"DPR is toast," I heard one of them mutter as he headed out the door.

His companion grinned. "We've got him now."

15: The Beating

Marriott City Center

It is interesting to me just how many Mormons are recruited into the higher echelons of police work. CIA, FBI, DEA, Secret Service—they all recruit heavily at Brigham Young University in part because Mormons tend to keep their noses clean, in part because many of them are bilingual, and in part because we tend to be patriots. I'm a bit disillusioned, but even I find myself wanting to make the system better rather than just tear it down.

I glanced around the circle of government agents. Their expressions didn't match the glee of the computer techs. In fact, some appeared solemn and others downright grim. Something tightened in my stomach, but I said, as lightly as I could manage, "Well, if we're finished, I need to call my wife to come pick me up." I looked hopefully toward Sherry from HLS. "Or does that offer of a ride home still stand?"

people who say, 'Hey, I'm missing half a bitcoin' after some transaction. There's not going to be a million dollars' worth of bitcoin in there, probably only a few grand worth."

Mr. Herring clearly wasn't listening to my argument. "You could have even done it this way," he insisted, and entered another rapid sequence.

I scrutinized the laptop screen and my brows scrunched. His new method had never occurred to me. "Oh. Yeah, you're right. I guess that is a way somebody could've done it—if they had a computer."

The other suits had stepped back, some with arms folded, some with hands in pockets, but all eyeing me. At my comment a couple of them traded conspiratorial glances. It didn't take much imagination to know what was passing through their heads: *Now* he's *thinking 'I wish I would've thought of doing that.'*

"I *didn't* steal anybody's money," I repeated in response to the doubtful expressions surrounding me. In truth, during my entire time working for Silk Road, it had never occurred to me to steal someone's money. And even, I suspect, if it had, I would have considered it to be too dangerous to even try.

"Why would DPR lie?" one man asked in a tone as stern as a disapproving father. He appeared to be a little older than most of the others, with gray at his temples.

Somebody else added, "Right. He has no reason to come up with a story like that."

Carl, I noticed, never chimed in. He just stood there watching me, somber-faced, with his arms crossed over his chest.

Justin persisted. The dark-haired HLS guy, the one who'd been so quiet over breakfast, jumped on me, too.

"I didn't do it!" I said again. "There's *no way* I could have stolen that money! I didn't even have access to a computer last night!"

"What about the computers in the business center at the hotel?" someone mentioned.

He was right, I could have gone there—if I hadn't been dead asleep.

My anxiety mounted as the crowd of government personnel seemed to close in around me. Their features had darkened like storm clouds rolling in over Utah Valley, laden with threat. My hands began to shake again, and my heart raced.

Now I've done it. Now they have reason to believe that I'm lying because I'm so upset.

Desperation mingled with lingering weariness, and my last emotional reserves collapsed like a flimsy dam during spring floods. I succumbed to tears.

Humiliation at my break-down kicked in a second later. Pressing a quivering hand to my streaming eyes, I shoved between the two figures blocking my way and stormed out of the room like a hormonal fourteen-year-old girl.

I barreled to the left down the posh hallway, not thinking at all about where I was heading. All I knew is I wanted out of there, to get away from everybody, to put space between myself and my interrogators until I could calm down and get myself under control.

The dense, soft carpet completely muted any footfalls, but I dimly heard a collection of voices rising behind me. A glance back revealed the whole pack of agents trailing after me.

Recalling it now, had I not been so upset, it actually would have been comical. All those men in their stiff, dark suits and ties chasing me like so many Keystone Kops. At that moment, however, only one thought shot across my mind.

They think I'm gonna bail. They think I'm gonna make a run for it. As if I could.

Breathing hard enough that I wondered if I'd start coughing up blood again, I stopped at the railing at the top of the staircase. I leaned against it, still sobbing, and jumped when a hand touched my arm. I spun around.

There stood Mr. Dark-Haired HLS Guy. "Back off, all of you," he ordered. He motioned sharply at the rest of the government herd, which had pulled up a couple of yards away. "Go away, will you, and give us some privacy."

Shooting quizzical, wary gazes from one of us to the other, they turned about one by one and started back the way we'd all come, but at a more-dignified pace.

As they retreated up the broad corridor, Mr. HLS returned his full attention to me. "Curtis," he began, in a tone he probably thought sounded sympathetic but came across to me as patronizing, "I know how you feel. You know DPR's a bad guy. He's a criminal and we want to get him. You know that. Just tell us. You can tell *us*. We won't hate you if you took that money. Come on now, Curtis."

A new idea crossed my mind. *Yeah, DPR's a bad enough guy that he could've stolen it himself, using my account info, to punish me for getting arrested or something. Have any of you geniuses considered that possibility?*

I didn't say it. I probably should have. Instead, as my weeping began to subside, I said, "Dude, I *didn't* take it! I had no means to do something like that. I can't tell you something that I didn't do. What else can I say to convince you of that?"

He didn't answer. He studied me for a moment, as if trying to figure out how to get me back into the emotional state of a few minutes earlier, but I shook my head. "Look," I said, "if I'd taken it, I would have told you so three hours ago. This is ridiculous."

We talked for several long minutes, and I don't think he ever really believed me.

When Mr. HLS and I reentered the suite, all the previously grim and threatening faces had become completely inscrutable. Carl crossed to me at once, but no one else spoke. They simply studied me. Shaun Bridges' gaze in particular seemed to bore straight into my soul.

"Listen, Curtis," Carl said, half aloud, "if you stole that money, it'll be a lot easier on you if just tell me."

I gaped at him in astonishment. In every one of his phone calls, every day since my arrest, he had been my biggest backer and most vocal supporter. "I believe you, Curtis," he had constantly said. "We'll get this worked out for you."

Now he's sided with my enemies.

"Carl," I said, "if I had stolen that money, I would've told you when you first mentioned it to me downstairs this morning."

He hesitated, but then he said, "DPR is pretty furious. He wants you beaten up and forced to return the stolen bitcoins." He said it with no hint of apology.

My eyes widened. "He *what?*" The words came out in a gulp. "Why didn't you tell me this before?"

He didn't answer that. Instead he said, "DPR wants photos. We'll just stage it, of course. What we're going to do is quasi-waterboard you, all right? Basically, we're just going to hold your head underwater so it looks like we're torturing you and take some photos."

Oh," I said. My voice sounded weak even to me. "Well, that sounds like fun. . ." *Not.* My heart rate quickened.

Carl ripped a page out of his notepad, pulled out a pen, and leaned over the table. I watched, knotting my hands together to stop their quivering, while he hastily scrawled a note.

"We need you to sign and date this," he said, and handed it to me.

I scanned it. Something to the effect that I voluntarily consented to allow the above-mentioned individuals to torture me and take photos as part of a sting operation against DPR. Or something like that.

Sherry, the blonde from HLS, read the page over my shoulder and rolled her eyes. "You're really lucky that we have Carl in charge of this," she said with a dim smile. "Could you imagine if he wasn't here and he hired somebody to beat you up that we couldn't control? We just need to keep up an appearance for DPR. We're actually doing this for your own safety, Curtis."

My own safety?

Somehow, I didn't find it very reassuring.

16: A Rough Baptism into the DEA (Reprise)

Marriott City Center

Drowning a man takes far longer than you would imagine. You need a good six minutes underwater. Carl Force and his men seemed to know that from personal experience.

Carl thrust his pen at me. I accepted it hesitantly and signed with a shaky hand.

Justin, the AUSA, had been growing increasingly uneasy during the last few minutes. I could see it in his face and in the way he paced stiffly at the edge of the cluster surrounding me.

"I can't be a party to this," he told Carl at last. "I can't witness this." And he left the suite.

I peered around after him. "Where is he going?"

They all appeared sheepish. Sherry stared at her shoes.

"He can't stay in here," Carl said, "because... our Mr. Herring is very by-the-book."

A huge, red flag immediately sprang up in my mind.

If Justin doesn't want to be a part it, that tells me they're doing something shady. Probably downright illegal.

I thought about saying, "I would like a copy of that note, please," but Carl had already tucked the signed paper inside his jacket. He motioned me toward the bathroom.

I walked in, and the rest of them followed.

For such an extensive suite, the bathroom seemed tiny. It certainly wasn't intended to hold five or six people at once. I stared at the bathtub, already filled with water.

Carl swished his hand in it. "Okay, I think I got the temperature about right. We'll need you to take off your shirt and kneel by the tub."

I unbuttoned my shirt with unsteady hands and peeled it off. I don't remember if somebody took it from me or if I just tossed it onto the bathroom counter before I eased myself to my knees on the cold, tile floor.

Carl had taken out his camera. I could tell it was a special model because everything on it appeared to be encrypted. Some kind of high-end digital type, kind of funny-looking and bigger than normal, with a bigger lens. It's odd how details like that stick so vividly in your mind when your adrenaline is ratcheted up.

Mr. Dark-Haired HLS Guy sat down on the edge of the bathtub. "Okay, Curtis," he said, "what I'm going to do is count to ten and then bring you up. If you need me to let you up sooner than that, just flail your arms."

"We're going to try to do this," Carl explained, "so it'll get a genuine reaction from you. That means you *will* experience some discomfort. Just a fair warning."

"Thanks," I mumbled. "I think."

Any movie director knows that real emotions can't be faked. It's easier to startle an actress, scare her, than it is for her to fake fear, and so directors often work to achieve "authenticity." It's a nasty practice in Hollywood. But that's what the police wanted to achieve here—the authentic look. It wouldn't be enough to try to fake my drowning, they needed to get me close to drowning and then "capture" that drowned look on film.

"All right, first shot, let's go," Carl said.

Mr. HLS Guy promptly seized the back of my head and shoved me into the tub with a splash that soaked me to the chest. With the water nearly to the bathtub's rim, he wouldn't have had to push very far to completely submerge my head, but he did anyway.

Without any warning, I had no chance to take a breath. Cool water flooded up my nose. All the way up, into my sinuses. I wanted to choke. I *needed* to choke.

Reflex made me try to flail, but I couldn't move my arms, due to my position and a very heavy hand gripping one of them. I felt another hand gripping the back of my undershirt.

By the time Mr. HLS Guy pulled me out, the distressed expression on my face was only partially from acting. I'm sure my eyes held all the desperation needed to convince DPR that I thought they were truly going to drown me.

While I coughed and gagged and tried to clear out the water I'd inhaled, Carl scrutinized his camera's display.

"So," I panted, once I got enough breath even to do that, "did you get it? I really don't want to do it again."

They eyed me, all four or five of them who were crowded into the bathroom behind me. I was soaked to the waist after one submersion, but the violent shaking that had seized me, like Max and Sammy on the day of the raid, had nothing to do with the chill of the air vents. They all stood over me, masked with those unreadable expressions.

They think I stole a million dollars.

It's just fake, I tried to convince myself. *I signed that waiver. They won't really drown me. They'd go to prison themselves and they know it. Don't be a wimp.*

"Hmm, not bad," Carl said, "but I think we should get a few more."

I was still wheezing and spluttering when Mr. HLS Guy's hand closed on my head again. I had just enough warning that time to gulp a small breath before my face met water.

With my ears submerged I couldn't hear whether anybody actually was counting out the seconds but doing it myself was the last thing on my mind. Kneeling on all fours, leaning into the tub as they had positioned me, I found my arms pinned once more. I couldn't get either of them free enough to even wave, let alone flail. All that pounded through my mind, over and over, was "I hope they bring me up soon, I hope they bring me up soon! I can't hold my breath for much longer!"

Of course it seemed longer that time, whether it really was or not. *It's got to be longer than ten seconds. I know it is! Are they really going to drown me?*

Opening my eyes didn't help. The smooth, pale bottom of the bathtub, so close to my nose, kicked in my claustrophobia.

I think they could tell I had panicked even without moving my arms. The hand lifted off my head. I came up puking water that time. It definitely felt a lot longer than ten seconds.

"You okay, Curtis?" somebody had the nerve to ask.

I couldn't speak. Too much water in my lungs. I shook my head and kept coughing. My lungs had been bleeding most of the week, but they hadn't hurt this bad.

"Let's get a few of him on the floor," another voice suggested. I don't know who said it, but I felt grateful for the brief reprieve.

They all backed away, enough for me to sprawl by the tub with my face lying in a puddle. That took some maneuvering and shifting around, partly for a good angle for their photos, but mostly because the bathroom was so ridiculously small.

"You need to look like you're scared to death," one of them told me.

Oh, I am *scared to death*, raced through my head, but I was still choking too much to say it. *Isn't that obvious?*

As I lay there trying to drag in some air, I overheard the others' chatter.

"Did you get it?"

"Got a good one that time?"

"What do you think? Good enough?"

Through water-blurred eyes I saw them passing around their cameras and cell phones to assess each other's shots. To my immense relief, none of them were laughing at my expense. Every face appeared deadly serious, all business, with scowling brows and pursed mouths.

". . . few more times," Carl said after a pause.

Why did they have to do it this way? I wondered. *Can't they just make up my face, you know, get my head wet and let me lie on the floor? Why can't they let me put my head under the water myself and have the guy just put his hand around my neck without pushing. There are so many ways they could have done this without actually doing it.*

The next time Mr. HLS Guy shoved me into the bathtub and I found myself nosing its hard floor, a new string of thoughts careened across my mind.

It feels like they're trying to get me to confess. They're trying to scare me into confessing that I did steal DPR's money.

I didn't mention that, even if I could have, when my "handler" pulled me out again. I was working too hard to draw a breath, for one thing. But I didn't want them to think that "maybe should I tell them" had even made a brief appearance in my mind.

I've already told them the truth. There's nothing else I can tell them.

I simply stared up at Carl from the floor. *Here I am, already soaking wet, coughing, choking, puking, and you want to take some more?*

I think they put me under five or six times before they decided they had enough photos. They took a few more of me lying on the floor looking half-dead, too.

"All right," Carl said at last. "You're good, you're good. We're done."

About time, I thought. *Any longer and I won't just look half-dead.* I felt half-dead.

I knew I had water in my lungs, and my heart pounded so hard and fast I wondered if I'd have a heart attack. All the shaking had left me weak with exhaustion, too. I needed help getting to my feet.

"I've got a plastic bag for your wet undershirt," somebody said, and held out the bag.

I peeled off my undershirt, wrung it out, and stuffed it into the bag. I grabbed one of the fluffy towels to dry myself from head to waist and accepted my dry shirt from someone else.

A glance at my watch told me that it was nearly ten; the "fake" drowning session had taken more than half an hour.

By the time I buttoned my shirt up and slogged back into the living room part of the suite, Justin had returned. He wore a very serious expression. "Have a seat, Mr. Green," he said, and pointed stiffly at a chair.

Now what? Aren't we done with this yet?

I sank into the chair, feeling limp, and the rest of my interrogators seated themselves as well, all facing me like some kind of tribunal.

This doesn't look good.

Justin eyed me closely for a couple of minutes, but the AUSA never asked about or commented on what had happened in the bathroom. I still detected uneasiness about that in the set of his face, and I thought, *What happens at the Marriott, stays at the Marriott. Sorry, Vegas.*

"All right, Curtis," he said, "you can go ahead and give us the details now."

"Details about what?" I asked.

I knew very well. *They still haven't dropped the idea that I stole all that money.*

It was late at night. I was felt hungry, exhausted, and had just gone through their little water torture session. For the next hour I felt like the prey in the middle of a feeding frenzy. Sharks in suits, all trying to get a bite of me. They approached the question from every conceivable angle, throwing out one question after another, and I knew they were trying to trick me into slipping and somehow incriminating myself.

"Dudes," I finally said, "I can't tell you something that I didn't do. I *couldn't* do it, I didn't have a computer last night. How many times do I have to tell you that?"

Justin blew out an exasperated breath. "Okay, have it your way, Curtis."

In the next instant he changed the subject. "There are only . . ." he counted the people in the room under his breath, "five people in the world who know who Carl is." He pointed a finger and glowered at me. "You're now one of them, so if there's a leak and they find out, we'll know that you did it."

They're finally coming clean that Carl is Nob?

I would have snorted and said, "It's about time," but I was still fitfully coughing up souvenirs from the dunking. I said instead, "How do I know that somebody's not going to go rogue? I can't."

"They won't do that," Justin said. "They know how critical it is to keep his cover."

I glanced at Carl, sitting next to Justin. He had his arms folded and hands knotted into fists again, and his jaw set hard. His eyes flashed a silent warning when I met them.

"Well, I sure won't say anything," I said. "That's all I can promise."

Justin gave a stiff nod. "Good," he said. "Just keep your mouth shut, Curtis. Carl will keep in touch with you as the case develops."

I wondered what they would do to me if Carl's cover got blown. I was already faced with drug dealers who thought I'd robbed them, and if his cover ever got blown, I wouldn't have friends on either side of the law.

I deliberately returned the conversation to the missing money. "Guys, I don't know why you don't believe me, but I'd be more than willing to take a lie detector test."

Justin arched an eyebrow. "Well, that's a possibility. We'll keep in contact."

"More than willing," I emphasized when he appeared to brush off my suggestion. "Look, I know I didn't do it. I'm not scared of taking the test."

He nodded tersely. "We know. We'll stay in contact."

I think that I was still in shock that night, or maybe I was just too exhausted and confused to think. But I kept wondering: DPR wanted me beat up so that I would return his million dollars—money that I didn't steal. Beating me up couldn't really accomplish anything, even if it was a fake beating.

    The only thing left to do is kill me.

17: The Drug Lords Line up to Kill Me

Spanish Fork, Utah

I've always believed that as Confucius suggested, "When others speak evil of you, the correct action is to live in such a way that no one believes the lies." It's hard to do that when you're dead.

It was after ten that night when the meeting finally broke up. Being mid-winter, it had been dark for five hours by then. Mr. HLS Guy, the water-boarder, ended up giving me a ride home.

He didn't talk much during the hour-long drive. Mostly he stayed as silent as he'd been at breakfast that morning. When he bothered to speak at all he sounded stern.

I got the impression that he'd joined Homeland Security for the same reason a lot of short, skinny guys join the military. He'd probably been one of those kids in high school who got beat up all the time, and now his profession gave him the chance to beat up on other people. Yeah, one of those jerks.

He allowed me to call Tonya during the drive, but I had to use his cell phone.

"I'm on my way home, Hon," I said. With a sidelong glance at my torturer, who kept his attention riveted on the road ahead, I added, "It wasn't much fun."

I saw his jerk mode come into play again when we got home. We'd scarcely entered the house and shut the door behind us when Mr. HLS lit into grilling Tonya.

I slipped her a glance as discreetly as I could. *I tried to warn you this might happen.*

Most of his questions to Tonya centered on the bitcoin machines. "When did Curtis order these machines? What are they used for? How long has he had them? Do you know how to operate them? How do you make money with them?"

Now, he'd heard all of my answers to these questions before, but I suspect that he thought I was lying, so he had turned it on Tonya.

It became clear pretty quickly that he wanted to find out if I'd gotten the bitcoin machines while I was working for DPR. If I had, I'm pretty sure that one or another of the agencies would have taken them all.

So I let Tonya speak. She hadn't been at our previous interrogations, but I knew she'd tell the truth.

I waited until Mr. HLS finally left at close to midnight to give Tonya the full account of what had happened that day. By then, in my state of exhaustion, my emotions lay just beneath the surface again. They broke through more than once as I described the experience.

I couldn't sit still while I talked. As I had through my night in the jail, I paced. My hands shook, my voice shook and broke, and I swiped repeatedly at moisture welling in my eyes.

"I don't know how they think I could've stolen that money," I said over and over, "but they wouldn't believe me."

Tonya's set mouth and flaring eyes revealed her fury at the situation. "First they steal *our* money from your belt-pack," she said, "and now they're accusing you of stealing from other people, too?"

She'd never forgiven the SWAT team for taking the cash I'd been wearing at my waist when they broke in.

Her expression widened to shock when I began to describe the water torture.

"They did *what?*" she demanded. "What were they thinking? Why couldn't they just get your hair wet? They could have drowned you!"

"I kept thinking one of those times they really would," I told her. "I know there's still water in my lungs."

"Maybe they should have," she said. "Look at the situation you've gotten us into! All of us!"

Tonya's anger with me, though completely understandable, was the hardest thing I'd had to bear to that point.

But there was more. She saw through the situation very quickly. "Look," she told me, "the only people who knew your logins were those cops on the task force. They're the ones who got access to Silk Road. It had to be one of them who stole the money!"

That idea shocked me so much, I couldn't believe it. I was raised in one of those small towns where the monolithic courthouse rose like a monument to justice. I couldn't see the truth just yet. But I began to suspect, just a little.

I went to my computer that night and double-checked some things. I remembered I had a few bitcoins in one of my online accounts. Sure enough, they'd all been cleaned out. Then I got thinking about an emergency Dwolla account, sort of like PayPal, so I checked my balance there. Sure enough, all of my emergency money had been stolen, too.

The very next day I got a call from Carl. Just about the last person on Earth I wanted to hear from. But Justin had said he would be in touch.

Can't I have even a few days' break from all of this?

Apparently not.

"Uh, listen, Curtis," he said. He sounded uncomfortable. The squirmy kind of uncomfortable you experience as a kid when you get caught doing something a parent or teacher has told you not to do. "I'm putting together this plan for you being kidnapped. What's going to happen is that starting tomorrow, you can't be seen. You can't be online, you can't go outdoors, you can't make phone calls. None of that."

"Why the hell not?" I demanded. I already suspected. I hadn't given back the money that I hadn't stolen, so someone wanted me dead.

He didn't answer my question. "Starting Monday, you *cannot* be seen," he reiterated. "Don't go outside, don't go near a window, do *not* leave your home. If you see anything suspicious, call me immediately. Call 911 if you need to."

"But—" I tried to interrupt. Our front door was still broken all to hell, and it wouldn't keep out a fly, much less a determined intruder.

"Be very aware of your surroundings, and of your family's surroundings," he went on, very firmly and without seeming to take a breath. "Just make sure you are gone. I can't emphasize that enough. You're *gone!*"

He continued to drill it into me. "Don't get online *anywhere*. Repeat after me, Curtis: 'I will not go outside. I will not contact anyone. I will not answer the phone. I will not go online.'"

Is that actually fear I can hear in his voice?

It sent one of those increasingly familiar prickles across my scalp.

"Carl, what the hell is going on?" I demanded.

At last I heard a pause from the other end. "Curtis," he said with great gravity, "you are supposed to be... well, gone."

He didn't use the word 'dead,' but he didn't have to. I got the picture loud and clear. That prickle in my scalp slid to a cold shiver down my spine. "Why?" I asked again.

I'm starting to sound like a persistent toddler.

When Carl answered I could tell he was fudging around. "We're still working out the logistics," he said. "I'm buying you some time. DPR has people following you."

"Following me?" I asked. *What people?*

This whole thing is starting to sound like some spy drama.

"For this week," Carl said, "you can still go out and about, but not next week. So, get everything done that you can ahead of time."

"Okay. . ."

I hung up the phone with my skin crawling. *It sounds like DPR has put out a hit on me. I told them he might do this when they first arrested me.* I wanted to know who he might have following me. Silk Road had plenty of ads for professional hitmen on it, and he might have gotten any one of those. Plus, DPR had personal contacts in several Latin American drug cartels. He'd even once told me that he thought that he might need some sort of "enforcers" in the future, and so he had reached out to the Hell's Angels and made contacts there.

I still didn't know which drug dealers had been robbed but knew that any one of them might want to rub me out.

The hit, I realized, might come from anywhere, and all of DPR's contacts would want to curry favor with him. I suspected that hitmen were lining up for the honor. Sometimes I hate being right.

18: The Proof of My Death is Highly Exaggerated

Spanish Fork, Utah

Saturday, February 16, 2013

I learned while working on the Silk Road: Never believe anything that you see on the Internet.

I knew that someone had put a hit out on me. I didn't know the details yet, only that I had been framed for theft by a cop, and that a cop had the money. I think that I was in shock for the first few days, but that turned into a sort of simmering rage.

Had DPR ordered the hit, or someone else? Which cop had gotten into the Silk Road Accounts and begun ripping off drug dealers?

I reasoned that whoever had gotten into the accounts would have raided some of the bigger clients. Those would most likely be the heaviest dealers—and the most dangerous.

We've all seen it on television shows like *Breaking Bad*—you screw with a drug dealer, and you're going to die.

I replayed the various possibilities in my mind. I remembered how the Homeland Security guy showed a certain genius for programming, and instant understanding of how to raid the accounts. Could he have done it? I didn't think so. He seemed squeaky clean.

Then there was the Assistant United States Attorney. I had a sort of instant dislike for him. He obviously thought of me as being the lowest kind of criminal, and I could tell that he'd written me off. I could call him worse things, but he was a jerk.

Then there was Carl Force himself. He'd seemed... quiet and withdrawn when the accusations were made, but he'd also assured me that he believed in my innocence—until we got to the stolen money. Then he'd been the first to badger me about the theft.

And there were others in the room—some who had kept silent, others who worked mercilessly to drag a confession out of me. To be honest, I didn't even know who to suspect.

My thoughts were a slow whirlwind, dancing around the topic.

Nor could I guess when a hitman might come knocking.

But as my anger raged, I realized something: I wanted to take down DPR and the crooked cops who'd screwed me. I wanted vengeance.

It's tough to get vengeance when you're supposed to be a corpse, so I began to watch, to study, and to wait...

Sometime in the middle of the next week, Wednesday or Thursday, Carl Force called again. I couldn't help feeling angry at what felt like his toying with me, but by then I felt more than a shadow of fear, too.

"Okay, Curtis," he said, his voice heavy with annoyance, though for once it didn't seem to be directed at me. "It looks like those water-torture photos we took last week aren't going to work. We need you to take some more, something more convincing."

"What do you mean by that?" I asked. Carl had never explained to me exactly how or when he had planned to use those shots from the Marriott.

"Well," he said, "we need a better photo. The ones we have aren't good enough. We can't see your face very well, and what we can see, you don't look... good enough."

You mean 'dead enough,' don't you? I thought. *No wonder you sound so uncomfortable, Nob.*

"So, okay, we need a picture of you in which your face is more prominent," he said. "We need you on the floor again, but this time make it look like you puked or something."

"All right..."

I knew that someone wanted me dead. I don't know why the cops didn't just pour ketchup on me and have me lying there with my tongue sticking out.

Tonya and I did the reshoot on Saturday, in our bathroom.

"They want it to look like you threw up?" she asked. "That's really strange." She crinkled her forehead and considered for a minute. Then she brightened. "Chicken & Stars soup! I'm pretty sure we've got a can or two around. Let me go check."

She returned a couple of minutes later carrying a classic red can of Campbell's best and a spoon. She stood there and shook her head while I pulled the tab and removed the lid from the can.

"Now, how are we going to do this?" she wondered aloud.

I studied the thick, yellow contents for a minute, then scooped out a spoonful and slopped it down the front of my undershirt. Tonya stared, aghast.

"This'll wash out, won't it?" I asked.

"It better, Curtis!"

Dribbling the condensed soup down my face with the spoon didn't create the desired effect.

"I think I'll just put some in my mouth and then spit it out," I said at last.

"Get down on the floor first," Tonya suggested.

I climbed down on my knees before I put a spoonful of the gelatinous soup in my mouth.

That proved to be a wise decision. There are good reasons why you add water to condensed soups. One is the consistency, not too different from a raw egg. The other, for some soups at least, is the high salt content.

I chewed on it a bit, to make sure that it looked as if the chicken and stars had gone down before coming back up. My gag reflex kicked in. I barely made it to my stomach on the floor before I had to spit it out. Heck, let's be honest. I kind of puked it up. I glimpsed the flash of Tonya's camera through the corner of my eye.

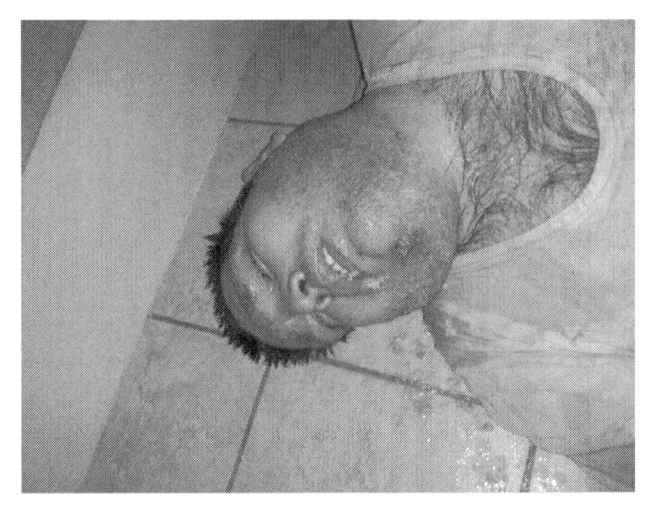

"Well, that looks really disgusting," she said a moment later, as she eyed her first effort. "I feel like we're shooting a scene for NCIS in our bathroom."

I remembered seeing an article in the paper about how one nearby special-effects company made props for dead bodies on the show, and wondered if I should give them a call and ask for a severed head or something.

"I wonder if they have this much trouble getting it right," I said from the cold tile. "I wonder what they use to simulate puke."

Tonya laughed. "Yeah, it can't make Mr. Campbell very happy to have his finest all over your shirt."

We took four pictures with me lying on the floor, soup oozing down my chin and my eyes half open. Keeping them half open and sufficiently blank was the tricky part. I kept needing to blink, and they naturally focused on Tonya.

If you've ever seen a real corpse, you know that getting the eyes right is tough. I wanted my eyes to be glassy, white, and just hoped that the people who wanted me dead wouldn't sweat the details.

Tonya used her Galaxy 4 cellphone, which took high-quality photos. We flicked back and forth through the shots a few times, chuckling at the images.

"You have no idea what Carl's going to do with these?" Tonya asked once. "Because this one in particular—" she paused on one pic, "—you really look like you've croaked!"

I think he's trying to keep me from becoming a dead body for DPR. That alone made me feel unexpectedly grateful to him. He was trying to save my butt, and I felt guilty for even suspecting that he might have stolen my money. Not super guilty, but a little.

I sent the photos off to Carl myself, straight from Tonya's cellphone.

A few moments later, a tone announced the arrival of a text message.

Carl had received our photographic adventure. "These are AWESOME!" he wrote. Yep, complete with caps and exclamation point. His excitement was palpable.

"Anybody would think we'd just won an Oscar," I grinned at Tonya.

I learned later that it was DPR who had put a hit out on me. He'd paid Nob $80,000 to do the job, and when DPR saw the photo of me as proof of a kill, he fell silent for several minutes, then wrote to Nob and said that he was "a little disturbed, but I'm ok. . . . I'm new to this kind of thing."

19: Observations from the Grave

Spanish Fork, Utah

For the past two years, President Trump has often decried "fake news." But sometimes when I look at our bungling bureaucracies, the way that we are promised things that never materialize, I want to point out that we have a "fake government."

On Monday morning, long before the late, winter dawn, we closed all the window blinds. I made sure everything was twisted tight, everything was pulled down. My personal state of siege, Carl's improvised in-house witness-protection program, had begun.

It felt more like house arrest to me. With the blinds drawn, our home remained semi-dark. It never really got light indoors, even with the bright, Rocky Mountain sunshine outdoors. Our weather in Spanish Fork stays sunny for 222 days per year, but for the next year, I wasn't going to get to see it once.

It was already mid-winter, and my mood sank to match my gloomy living conditions almost immediately. Some days, in my anxiety over my impending fate, I paced the hallway outside our bedroom for up to twenty hours straight, until my legs ached, and over the next year I lost nearly a hundred pounds.

I couldn't help wondering if DPR had hired a private investigator to make sure I really was dead.

Of course, my wife and kids had to go along with the charade. Tonya reported me "missing" to the police and made sure that she didn't wear a smile in public.

A couple of weeks into my indoor exile, in late February or early March, someone came to the door and asked for me. The woman carried a piece of paper, a notebook, and a pen, and she specifically asked where I was.

My daughter Tiffany answered the door. With an appropriately distressed expression on her face, she said, "Oh, he's not here. We don't know where he's at."

I actually saw the visitor. I came sneaking out and peeked around the corner and got a split-second glimpse. I could tell it was a woman by the way she stood and how she spoke.

When she left, Tiffany told me, "Yeah, she asked for you by name."

Tiffany handled it perfectly, but it still freaked me out. *That's really weird. It doesn't sound right.*

Feeling suspicious and more than a little nerve-racked, I immediately called Carl.

He proceeded to grill me. Did she ask where you were? Did she ask for a phone number? What exactly did she want?

I gave him all the information I could, everything Tiffany had told me about the encounter.

"I don't think you have anything to worry about," he said at last. "Didn't you tell me you were behind on your mortgage payments?"

"Yes, we are," I replied. "About three months." I'd hoped to use my $20,000 tax refund to pay the mortgage, but that was all gone, and our efforts to get it back from the government were all coming up empty.

My lawyer had been in touch with the AUSA and had even requested the $3000 stolen from my Dwolla account, thinking perhaps that it had been seized, but the AUSA didn't seem to understand that the money was gone. I don't think he ever did figure out that I'd been robbed of it.

"Three months?" Carl said. "That sounds about right. When people get far enough behind on payments, say three or four months before they go into foreclosure, all the realtors know about it. I think she was probably just a realtor." But he added, "Still, keep your eyes open. Next time somebody comes to the door, have your wife or daughter ask for a business card."

In my physical isolation, I couldn't resist going back on Silk Road. I knew I wasn't supposed to. Carl had been explicit. But I wanted to see what people were saying. I wanted to find clues to the crime.

Both of my Silk Road accounts, as Chronicpain and Flush, had been shut down, but I didn't have to log on. You can go to the site without logging in. You only need to login to leave a post, and I certainly wasn't going to do that.

What really drove me back to Silk Road was curiosity about the so-called theft. What were people saying about it? I searched for quite a while, but not one of the posts I read was from anybody complaining about, "Hey, I'm missing some money!"

That raised more questions for me.

Did the theft really even happen? Did DPR make up the whole story about it? Or did Carl and his little government friends come up with that tale themselves?

I felt used and furious. A certain low-level, smoldering anger joined my depression.

Carl had allowed me to continue with my job, the one that involved taking calls and doing customer service for the a non-profit organization. "Yeah, I guess you can do that," he said.

"Well good, because I don't have much choice," I told him. "It's my only source of income now." Two thousand a month wasn't much, so Tonya went to work as a manager at a local convenience store.

While at work, I never answered the phone as myself, however. Whenever a caller asked for my name I gave a fake one, a regular, familiar name like Mike or Steve or John, whatever happened to be passing through my head at the moment.

Worry hovered over me, along with my anger with Carl. I pre-positioned our handguns at strategic locations around the house and made certain that Tonya knew where they were. I put one in the kitchen, and one on each side of the bed in our bedroom.

I also brought in baseball bats from the garage and placed them at critical spots throughout the house. We had lots of baseball bats. Tonya had coached our church's girls' softball team for a while.

I propped one of them in the corner behind the still-broken front door.

I feel like a caveman, I thought, hefting it. *But if that's what it takes. . .* The bat felt comforting and dangerous in my hand. I thought, Never bring a gun to a baseball-bat fight.

The dire tone of Carl's warnings lingered, haunting me. I stayed in the house always, in the dark. I only came out to the kitchen at night. Even then, I crawled up the stairs and to the sinks, not wanting to be spotted through the windows. I avoided opening the refrigerator. I never even peeked through the blinds.

You might feel safe in your own house in the dark, but that is an illusion. There are night-vision goggles that you could buy on Silk Road, and I wondered if you could buy infrared goggles—the ones that made your body heat show up like a flare at night, even through walls.

It's like being Dracula from some old movie.

I should point out that I wasn't forgotten. Carl continued to call me at least once a day, often twice, and sometimes he would stay on the phone for hours.

"Anything new?" he always asked, until it almost became a mantra: Anything new, anything new, anything new?

He wanted to "make sure you're cool," he always said. "You're not in touch with DPR? Not in touch with anybody coming by the house?"

It got to the point that he started sounding like an audio recording, and I turned it right back on him. "Yes, yes, no, no," I'd respond.

I don't know whether he was legitimately concerned about my safety. I never could tell. I couldn't help wondering if he was really more concerned about developing his case against DPR. But I certainly had concerns. I brought it up to him more than once.

"How worried should I be, Carl? Just be honest and upfront with me."

"Well," he finally said, "there's a scale we've used to analyze mob activity for years. They give it a number. When we did the threat evaluation on you, it was so low that it barely registered. I don't think you have anything to worry about. But play it safe. Keep your nose clean and your head down, that sort of thing. We're pretty sure there are eyes on you."

Eyes on me. Great.

To be honest, I felt more worried for Tonya and the girls than for me. We still hadn't been able to afford to get that door fixed, and our house payments were slipping further behind, getting closer to foreclosure.

Tonya and the kids were worried, too. Amanda quit bringing our grandson over. It was too dangerous.

Mostly I hung out in our bedroom watching TV, whatever happened to be on at the time. Game shows, how-to shows, sports, soap operas, evening dramas. I wasn't picky. I had too many hours to kill. I couldn't do much to work out, except pace. I wore a path in our carpet.

Sometimes I gave in and got on the internet, but I stayed away from any site with a chat capability. That would expose me in a heartbeat.

I actually went to Bitcoin Talk once, where I had spent so many hours learning about bitcoin mining and bitcoin commerce before I found Silk Road. I talked to the moderator, the guy in charge.

"I can't tell you what's going on," I said, "but can you change my user name to this," and I gave him a new one, "just in case?"

I don't think anyone knew my old username, but by then I'd seen too many things done online that I have no idea how they figured out. I felt grateful when he went ahead and changed my username for me without asking questions.

Bitcoin Talk was the main website that I went to. But from time to time I also checked out KSL.com and Fox News. Google became my encyclopedia.

While I was in hiding, I really couldn't do much investigating on my own, I discovered. I couldn't ask questions of people I knew.

Carl's nightly calls were my main source for news. I felt reliant on him, and I suspect that Stockholm Syndrome set in, where a captive begins to sympathize with his captors.

We would chat for long hours. Sometimes he would call from his home, and I could hear his small children playing in the background. Once he called and talked in whispers while he was at a late-night stakeout.

Almost from the very first, I took him into my confidence. I wondered which of the cops had stolen the money from the dealers on the Silk Road and ran options past him. He said that he didn't know but urged me to trust only one person: Shaun Bridges. "We're tight, he and I. You're going to get calls from a lot of people—FBI, Homeland Security. But only talk to me or Shaun. He can be trusted."

And Shaun did call later that day and asked questions about how to transfer bitcoins from one account to another, how to hide them, and how to cash them out. I told him how he could take his bitcoins offline and put them on a flash drive, so that you could be walking down the street with a hundred million dollars in your pocket and no one would ever know, until you put those bitcoins on a computer. In short, he was asking good questions: if you were a cop trying to catch dealers, and it was much the same kind of information that I talked about with Carl on his daily calls.

So sometimes Carl and I discussed bitcoin, but normally we talked about the usual things—our families, the cases he was working on. He told me once about how he was going to be busting a nasty murderer and drug dealer, and I urged him to be careful.

There was a duplicity to his tone though, I noticed. Sometimes when he called me from the office, he would become all business and say in a firm voice, "Now I want you to come clean here! You've got to give back that money you stole."

But when he was at home or in his car, he sounded conciliatory. "I believe that you didn't steal the money, Curtis, but no one else does. I *know* you didn't steal it."

I was mad, of course. Whoever had stolen the money had framed me for the theft, and at first, I wondered if the police were just trying to force me into cooperating. That's how it is done on television. The cops do something that will get a witness killed and then coerce them to testify.

The only thing was, I had already been cooperating fully when the money was stolen.

No, whoever had stolen the money, I reasoned, did it out of pure greed. By framing me, it almost seemed that they wanted to see me executed. That way, the cops would figure that I'd stolen the money and close the investigation.

So, the thief who framed me was a stone-cold killer who would just let someone else do the wet work.

I figured that the thief wanted me out of the way precisely because I knew how Silk Road worked, and they were afraid that I would figure out what was going on. If I died, I'd be out of his way, the Feds would think that I'd stolen the money and that the account info was forever lost, and he'd be in the clear.

I agonized over who could have done this, but I had too many suspects and not enough access to Silk Road. I couldn't go online, didn't dare blow my cover. All I could do was wait.

There were some anomalies over the months. For example, once Carl called and asked me about bitcoin mining. He said that he was buying some computers and wanted to know which would be best. That seemed very "off" to me at the time. I couldn't figure out how he would have so much money to invest in bitcoin. Yet he often asked about how cryptocurrencies worked or which way I thought the currency would move. He wanted to know when to jump in, and when to pull out, and he sought details on how to find the exchanges that would let him turn his bitcoins into cash.

He also tried to bring me closer to him. He asked several times if I would come to Boston so that I could "help out" on some cases. It sounded like promising a job offer, and I felt eager to do it, to redeem myself, but my defense attorney strongly warned against it. After all, I still had charges pending against me, and my attorney worried that I might say something that would be used against me in court. She said, "You'll go to Boston over my dead body!"

So, I had an abundance of tedium in my life. Tonya often brought in food when she went out for one thing or another, and we ordered out a lot. We had a Café Rio right down the street, and a Mongolian barbecue nearby. "Eating out" was pretty much my only source of excitement.

Café Rio, a fresh-Mex place, is good, but I particularly like the Mongolian. You choose noodles, meat, vegetables, and seasonings from a setup like a buffet, load them into a bowl, and they fry it for you. In the past we had always stood there and watched the cooks do it, stirring our ingredients around and flipping them over on the large, smooth grill. In my housebound state, I could only imagine them doing it every time I opened the delivery package and inhaled the mingled aromas.

In his daily calls, Carl informed me that he was talking to DPR on a regular basis. "The photos you sent made a deep impression," he told me once. From that I gathered that DPR truly believed me to be dead. I guess Carl thought hearing that would bring me some relief.

"We've taken some measures," he once said. "I can't tell you what we're doing, but just to let you know, we're doing some things to make you safer."

"Well, what *are* you doing?" I insisted. I suspected that he was just trying to calm me down, not that he was really doing anything.

"I can't tell you that," he repeated. "You could still be one of the bad guys."

I snorted. "Carl, get off that, you know better. You know very well I'm not with anybody. Don't insult my intelligence."

"Sorry," he said. But he still didn't tell me.

Carl, my only source of information on the case, seemed to have dried up.

Looking back, I remember the old saying from the movie the Godfather, "Keep your friends close, and your enemies closer." I believe that that's what Carl was doing, trying to wring any information from me that he could.

That was sometime in April. For that first month, I didn't dare open the curtains, and I didn't answer the door, and I often let phone calls pass, if I didn't recognize the number. Even now, years later, I keep the curtains drawn and feel a little prick of panic when the doorbell rings.

But at that time, I put the guns and baseball bats away. It wasn't that I felt safe. It's that Tonya and I talked, and we both decided that we were tired of being scared. If we got killed, then fine. There wasn't much we could do to stop it. We refused to live in fear anymore.

Nothing's most likely going to happen, I told myself.

Somewhere along the line Carl suggested that I move—just pack up and leave my house. I think that he felt it was *that* dangerous.

He then put me in contact with a woman who handled a Witness Protection Program.

Great, give me a mortgage, I thought. *I'm so out of here.*

I didn't really expect the government to give me a house, but I thought that if they could pay a new mortgage for a bit and move us, hell, I'd go to Wyoming. I'd go wherever they sent us.

It turned out that wasn't quite the case. The government only offered to pay my moving expenses, and even those were minimal. They'd pay for me to rent a U-Haul, basically. No down-payment for an apartment, no job or change of name, none of the stuff that you see them do in movies. I guess I wasn't important enough for them.

"What?" I said. "If that's all we get, there's no way I can afford to move. I'm paying three percent interest on my house. I won't be able to get a house loan like that again."

"Well," the woman said, "if you're not willing to move, we think prison is your best option. You'll be safer there." It felt like an ultimatum: Leave me alone or go to prison, I don't really give a damn which you choose.

"You're kidding me," I said again. "They'll get me easier in prison than they will out here."

So much for that option.

Somehow, I kept feeling that someone was trying to get me killed: the frame-up with the cocaine, the thefts from the drug dealers that led to the hits, the government's refusal to protect me. It was all adding up. Even the idea of going back to Boston seemed dangerous, since it would leave me far from home in a strange place, where a hitman might find me.

It wasn't just me and my defense attorney who were worried. I think in the end it was Tonya, who just felt that going to Boston would leave me open to another setup.

20: Seasons in the Dark

Spanish Fork, Utah

June 2013

Seasonal affective disorder, or SAD, causes a lot of people to become moody or depressed in the fall and winter. I sometimes wonder if some chemical gets sent to their brain by mistake, so that they are like bears going into a false hibernation. But when you're stuck in a house with the blinds drawn and the lights off, it can last all year.

I didn't get to go outside at all for the next four months. When at last I did, it was only for an appointment with an attorney, Mr. Ron Yengich. I finally had called him, and he was angry that I hadn't phoned earlier. I really didn't have any choice but to go to him, even though he knew I was supposed to be "playing dead." He wouldn't come to me.

I'd been shut in for months. In the Mormon Church, there are organizations that help those who are sick or suffering, but in my case, I had become a pariah. None of my old friends had called or come over to visit, even though my wife supposedly had a dead husband and was "grieving."

And in fact, she was in mourning—not for me, but for the life that we had lost. Our daughters were afraid to even come to the house, and so she seldom got to see our grandson.

One day the doorbell rang, and my heart started thumping. My wife answered, and it was two city policemen. They questioned her for about half an hour, asking if she had any idea where I might have disappeared to. She told them no, while I listened to them talk from the darkness of the stairwell.

Later that afternoon I told Carl about their visit. He was the one who had turned in the false report, and I'd learned that it was illegal for him to do so. Now we had local cops wasting time, searching for my body.

But Carl thought it was for the best. He said that he didn't know what kinds of resources DPR might have, what informants he might have access to, so it was best if even the cops thought I was missing.

Staying inside for months wore on me, so going out on that bright day turned out to be easier than I thought it would be. I stepped out the front door in broad daylight, and felt fully prepared for a bullet to take me.

Early summer had come to Spanish Fork by then. The days had grown long, the last snow had melted except on the tallest of the mountain peaks, leaving the normally tan mountainsides a new green. The neighborhood lawns had also grown green once more, and the hummingbirds and monarch butterflies had returned from their sojourn somewhere to the south.

I blinked at the brightness for several seconds, until my eyes adjusted, and almost recoiled when a summer breeze swept my face.

Weird. I've actually forgotten what wind in my face feels like. How could that happen?

The attorney's office was located in Salt Lake City, a drive of fifty miles. I had been hoping to obtain a high-profile attorney because my appointed defense attorney had proven to be mostly useless.

Now, I say that she felt useless, but maybe that's not quite fair. I felt that Mary seemed to dislike me. She acted as if she was sure that I had stolen the money and was an active drug dealer, and she even begged me to "come clean" and throw myself on the mercy of the court. She pressured me to return the stolen money so much, I even considered "confessing" and offering to repay the money, just to get her off of my back. She kept warning me that if I didn't, I could be sent to prison for the rest of my life.

Every time that I suggested that we do something to prove my innocence, to prove that I had been set up, she gave me a disbelieving stare, almost as if she wanted to roll her eyes. I felt as if she just wanted me to quit bothering her.

The problem was, I really couldn't afford an attorney. I was advised that if I hired a good defense attorney, it would cost me about $300,000 just to get through the trials. But at the time, my home was in foreclosure and I had almost no income at all, since I was supposed to be dead, and of course the government had seized all my money, and some cop had stolen even my bitcoins and my cash account.

The funny thing is, if I'd actually been the big drug dealer that they accused me of being, I might have actually made enough money for my own defense.

As it was, I was hoping to get a high-profile attorney and then borrow the money to pay him from a wealthy uncle.

So, I went to Salt Lake to meet with Ron Yengich; he was regarded as the highest-profile criminal attorney in Utah, and his office stood smack in the middle of downtown Salt Lake. Probably within sight of the Marriott, where I'd been water-tortured in January.

The thought of being in downtown Salt Lake again gave me a shudder. I felt thankful that my father had offered to drive me there.

That was probably most appropriate, looking back, because Mr. Yengich had been recommended to my father by one of his friends who was also an attorney. "He's won cases that appear to be unwinnable," my father's lawyer friend had told us.

Our get-acquainted session lasted about an hour, but I didn't pay attention to any clocks. The old anxiety was settling in once more.

It didn't help that my father sat in on the meeting rather than waiting out in the lobby. After the introductions were made, my father didn't speak at all, but I saw tautness in his features and in the way he moved, and I felt stress emanating from him as he sat.

Ron Yengich listened patiently, his elbows planted on his redwood desk's vast top and his fingers steepled, as I told my story. As much of it as I could tell in an hour, anyway, and as much as he would be able to argue before the Supreme Court of the District of Maryland. He studied me from beneath bunched brows and pursed his thin mouth the whole time.

When I finished, he leaned back in his black-leather chair and eyed me sternly over the tops of his glasses. "It's always the damned internet," he said, and shook his head. "When will you kids learn to leave it alone?"

Kid? I thought with some indignation. *He's calling me a kid? I'm practically fifty!*

"I represent a number of child pornographers," he explained, almost as if it were an apology. "The internet is where they were first exposed to it."

I squirmed in my deep, padded chair like a schoolboy called to the principal's office and stared at my shoes. The waves of tension rippling off my father seemed to triple, as if he'd been called in for a parent-principal meeting about my misbehavior on the playground.

At last Mr. Yengich sighed deeply, shook his head once more, and leaned toward me over his desk. "Well, let me look into the case," he said. "I've got a few colleagues in Maryland that I can check with. I'll call you back in a few days and let you know if I can take your case."

If *I can take your case? That's not reassuring.*

I wondered what was wrong. Mr. Yengich handled most high-profile cases in Utah, and I'd hoped that mine would be an easy win for him, but he sounded... unsure.

My mood, teetering on the edge already, dropped through the figurative floor as we left his office.

"Do you want to get lunch or run any other errands while we're in Salt Lake?" my father asked. His voice remained crisp and stern.

We had talked about it on the drive up. We'd planned to do lunch at a good restaurant, when we set out in the morning, but my heart wasn't in it. I felt as if I didn't have anything to celebrate.

"I just want to get home," I told him.

He didn't say anything, though he studied me for a moment.

Does he have any idea how extremely depressed I am? The months in darkness seemed to sap the life out of me, but it was far more than that. The worry, the despair. Every time that I felt I was making progress, it seemed that I got knocked back on my butt again. I was trying to figure out how to scrape myself up off the ground.

I don't know if he picked up on it or not. I just know that we drove in silence.

21: Regretting My Deal with the Devil

Spanish Fork, Utah

Summer 2013

Life sometimes forces you to choose between two evils. Usually we try to choose the lesser of two evils, but next time I'm given that choice, I think I'll go with the most interesting evil.

The last time I'd been so happy to see my home was the day I'd been released from jail. The front door didn't hang on its hinges this time when my father and I pulled into the drive, since I'd finally scraped together the thousand dollars to get it fixed.

To my surprise, even after months of being confined to the house, I couldn't wait to get back inside.

It's funny how that works. When you're stuck in one place for a long time, no matter how uncomfortable, it begins to feel like home. I remembered the man in the County Jail who wanted to stay. I practically sprang from the car to the front step.

I had to leave the house only a couple more times during the next few weeks, both times for doctor's appointments. My weight fluctuated dramatically during my house imprisonment. First, I had gained about a hundred and fifty pounds in the last few years, then lost it all again as I paced the floors, wearing a trail in our carpet.

Definitely not healthy.

My mental health was in bad shape, too. I'd been downing anti-anxiety pills as if they were popcorn during that time, so my doctor prescribed some medication for the depression.

The lawyer I had staked so much on, Mr. Yengich, never did call back.

Well, I thought morosely, *it looks like he didn't want my case.* I didn't want to go crawling to him. When you've got nothing left but a little pride, it feels more precious.

After a few weeks I called my father, just to be sure that he hadn't heard anything. "Dad, has Yengich called back yet?"

"No," my father replied, "he's never called me. But he said he would call us, regardless."

Feeling dejected, I decided to see if I could find a new high-profile attorney. My father told me that one of the best was Scott Williams, so I made some phone calls and found that I like him.

Now, let me be clear. There were two Scott Williams's in the phone book. One was a high-profile criminal attorney, and one was much less experienced. When I made my phone call, it was my luck to get the wrong one. Maybe that was a happy accident, because I really like my Scott Williams. I finally felt that I found someone who believed in me, who would stand up for me.

At first, I was willing to go into debt and pay for him to be my defense attorney, but the government soon made him my official attorney.

So, I went to see my public defender. She'd set up a phone meeting with AUSA Justin Herring in San Francisco, and my attorney wanted me to be there to hear Herring's offer as they bargained for my future.

I dragged myself out of the house for a second trip to Salt Lake City. Once again, I was accompanied only by my father, but this time we took the light-rail train that crisscrosses parts of the Wasatch Front.

I was feeling pretty optimistic about the deal, so we sat down while my new attorney prepared to make his call to the AUSA. He warned me that it was a bit unusual for me to sit in on this call, so he warned me to not say a word, to not even breathe hard, while we were on the call, then he punched in the numbers. He had laid out a sheaf of papers across his broad desk, probably to make them easier to read from our seats facing him.

I wasn't expecting a *great* deal, like a proverbial slap on the wrist, though a few months of probation had been mentioned by several people. Carl Force repeatedly said that I'd get something like that, since I'd helped so much with the investigation, but those thoughts had been echoed by FBI agents and others.

So I certainly wasn't expecting the offer from the AUSA. "We think we can limit the sentence to a maximum of forty years."

Forty years. My mouth dropped open. *Forty years!*

Even though I had heard the grim figures before, I was in shock. I'd been framed, had my money stolen. I'd signed a proffer agreement and had done everything that the AUSA asked, and now he said they'd "limit" it to forty years?

What about the bargain he'd made?

I went numb with shock and couldn't even think.

The news didn't completely sink in, however, until we'd left my defense attorney's office. About the time we reached the elevator. I stopped short and stared, at what I don't know. The abyss. I was peering into the abyss, and all of it was dark.

Forty years! All the cops were talking probation, and this is what I get? What about that proffer agreement?

Forty years! I never even bought or sold any drugs. Anyone would think I'd killed somebody.

I still held the papers in my hand. Crushed in my hand. I had been reading them because my attorney had said, "You need to go through these documents with a fine-toothed comb."

My father stood watching me. "How much of this is true?" he demanded. "What parts of it aren't true?"

I shook my head. "None of these charges should be in here," I said. "I had the proffer agreement deal to drop the charges if I helped them make a case. But they're going for the max. The name "Chronicpain" should not even be in the indictments. I signed the agreement before they even learned of that name."

Flashes of the conversation replayed in my mind. "They're not going to let it go," my attorney Scott had warned.

I had grown impatient. "That's why you go to a judge and tell them you know what really happened," I insisted. "We need to get a judge to decide. You don't just take what the prosecution offers you."

The elevator door shushed open and we stepped inside. I couldn't stop staring at the papers crumpled in my hands, as the elevator began to descend.

Forty years? The words kept repeating in my head, like a drumbeat inside my skull.

I began to tremble. I could feel it through my whole body, especially in my knees, but my hands shook so badly that they made the clenched papers rattle.

The elevator came to a stop with a small bump, and I swayed. As I stepped out, I put my hand on my father's shoulder to steady myself.

He glared at me and brushed my hand away with a sharp motion.

The same tidal wave of emotions that had buried me that day in the Marriott, the emotional wall that had pushed me out of the suite and down the corridor with a gaggle of government agents trailing behind, crashed down on me again. I succumbed, as I had then, to tears.

"Oh, shut up, Curtis," my father said. The words came in a furious hiss through his clenched teeth. "Shut up and take it like a man!"

I looked up. Several people moved around the main lobby, most of them well-dressed and making their way briskly, as if to keep appointments. None of them so much as glanced in our direction, and yet my father was obviously humiliated.

He doesn't want to be seen with me, the alleged online drug-dealer in the family, by anyone he knows.

That thought wracked another sob from my chest.

He shoved through the building's front door well ahead of me, striding quickly, as if to put distance between us. I blinked as I followed him out of the vast, dim and air-conditioned lobby into the bright heat of the Rocky Mountain summer. I had to hurry to keep up.

"You'd better not cry on the train," he shot over his shoulder.

I didn't answer. I couldn't. A painful knot had clogged my throat. Sometimes, I learned, the ability to "cowboy up" eludes you.

We waited on the platform without a word between us. I kept my wet eyes focused on that sheaf of damning papers; he kept his head up and his gaze narrowed in the opposite direction.

I'm going to go through all of this, trying to work it out. I'm going to have to do it alone.

More of Scott's word replayed in my mind, "Justin is gonna put you in prison. You know that, right?"

And I'd answered, "No, I'm not going to prison. I'll kill myself before I go to prison."

Scott tried to reassure me. "Prison, well, prison is not that bad. It's a learning experience, so you can make yourself better." He tried to turn it into a positive. He told how one of his best friends is an attorney that got sent to a prison, and he's now out and he actually has his law license back. He was trying to show me the positives.

I told him how Carl at the DEA wanted me to work for him, so I suggested, "Hey, instead of me going to prison, let's work out a deal. I'll work for them for years, something like that." I pressed him, "Come on, let's use our heads here, people. I'll work for three years without pay, without. . . Come on, if they need my help, let's go for it."

I was in a trap, and I knew it. The prosecutors weren't going to honor their agreement. Even though I had been completely honest with them, all that they had to do to annul the agreement was to pretend that they didn't believe me.

I think then that I began to realize that I would be going to prison for a very long time.

As we left the attorney's office, the rigid figure of my father at the edge of my vision, aloof and deliberately ignoring me, swept me with a greater loneliness than if I had been standing there by myself.

What does it matter? I thought. *If I see somebody crying, I just think they must be having a bad day. Maybe their child is sick and they're worried. Maybe they just lost a loved one. You look around and make sure everything's okay with them. I don't think badly of them. It's a human emotion. People cry all the time. That's life.*

My father, however, has never seemed to have any emotions, even when all of us were small. At least, if he has emotions he doesn't know how to show them.

When my breath caught again, in my efforts to suppress my weeping, he glared at me. "Just shut up. Come on, good grief!"

I'd brought a lot of embarrassment on my family. I'd known that from the moment the SWAT team busted down my front door. I'd lived with it every single moment since. And it killed me, especially for my family's sake.

If I could give my life to take it away, Dad, I would. But I can't. It hurts to know you're not behind me. You don't seem to get that. Nobody seems to get it.

In October I was officially charged in Federal Court. They said that I had to go to Baltimore to see the judge. I couldn't figure out why I had to go all the way to Baltimore, when I lived in Utah.

The government was even willing to pay my way—so long as I rode in a bus. The idea was that it would go all day, then stop for the night, where I would get off and be checked into a nearby jail or prison. The travel time might take most of a week.

I asked if I could just fly instead, but they said that the government wouldn't pay for that. Now, that didn't sound like it made any sense to me. How would it be cheaper to have cops pick me up at a bus station every night, process me into the jails, and then deliver me to the bus station every morning? Couldn't they fly me there for a third of that price?

I was told that I could indeed fly, but I would have to pay my own way. I considered my back and the pain that taking this bus would cause, and opted to fly myself out. The court of course was happy to fly my attorney out for free.

When I got to Baltimore, the judge read the official charges, promptly sealed the indictment so that it wouldn't be leaked and sent me back to await trial.

I didn't leave the house again after that.

22: Waiting for Justice

Spanish Fork, Utah

Winter and Summer of 2013

You can spend your life hoping for justice. Ultimately, it will never come.

For the next few weeks I became reconciled to the notion that I was going to lose everything.

I worked with my new attorney to get the money that had been seized back, but the AUSA was slow to let me have it. After all, I suspect he reasoned, if I had money, I could actually pay for a defense. So, he was trying to starve me into a confession.

I spent days replaying incidents in my mind, the talks with Carl Force and Shaun Bridges. I knew that a cop had stolen the money, but my good friend Carl had convinced me to look at other suspects.

The offers of a job even began to sound more sincere, more imminent, but Carl said that the DEA couldn't bring me on until after my case had been adjudicated.

So I simmered. When you're frustrated, unable to move forward, to progress, the frustration eventually turns to anger, and I had begun to grow angry. The shock and disbelief at my situation had faded away, and even though I still lived in hiding, I felt that I was doing that in part for my wife and family. Yet I felt an urgency to solve this case, to get my pound of flesh.

Sometime in July, the ASIC machines I had purchased in June the previous year were finally delivered. I turned my attention completely to unpacking them, setting them up in my basement, and putting them to work at bitcoin mining. At last I had something better to do than watch TV.

If I'm going away to prison for forty years, I've got to make sure Tonya and the girls are taken care of. Those machines became sort of an insurance policy.

Tonya no longer griped about my bitcoin mining. In fact, she often passed by my chair, rested a hand on my shoulder, and asked, "How are we doing? What are bitcoins worth today?"

"We're doing fine," I said. "I'm going to get you a new car, Hon." And after a few months I got her a nice reliable Honda. She'd taken a job, and I figured that she might need transportation for the next decade or two.

The summer passed, fading into fall, but I didn't see the changing leaves on the mountainsides. I may have put the guns and bats away, but I remained confined to the house.

I also remained cautious about going online. I limited my visits to the sites I knew, mostly those involved with bitcoins and mining, and even when I used them, I visited under a pseudonym.

On the morning of October 2nd, the top stories running on Fox News were the impending government shutdown, and Israeli Prime Minister Netanyahu's speech before the UN. While the news anchors murmured in the background and flashed pictures of the U.S. capitol building and clips from Netanyahu's speech, I got onto the BTC-e website, a company that exchanged bitcoins. Theirs was one of the few chatrooms I still followed regularly. I felt confident my identity was still safe there.

I'd only been on BTC-e for a few minutes when someone posted an announcement that rocked me back in my chair.

"Silk Road just got busted. There's an FBI sign that comes up when you try to log in."

Holy shit!

When I searched the web, it was breaking news. The FBI said that they had arrested Ross Ulbricht, age 29, in a coffee shop in San Francisco. The pictures of him showed a nice-looking kid, handsome with brown hair and penetrating eyes, the kind of young man that I'd hope my daughter might marry. Nothing on his face would indicate that he had a secret life as a murderer and a drug dealer and the kingpin of one of the world's largest crime empires.

I admit it, I freaked out. "Oh, yeah!" I yelled. "You gotta be kidding!" I'd known they would bring DPR down eventually, but somehow it felt as if it would never come. I jumped to my feet and yelled again, "You gotta be kidding me!" I glanced around. "Tonya? Are you in the house?"

She came dashing into the bedroom, her expression panicked. "Curtis? What's wrong?" she asked, a split second before she saw my beaming face.

"Nothing's wrong. They got him! They just caught DPR!" I pointed at the news story on my computer monitor.

She stared. "Oh, my word! Oh, my word, Curtis, that's amazing!" She let it sink in for a moment, and then suddenly her eyes became moist with tears and she laughed with relief as she cried.

"I've got to call my brother Darren," I said. "I've got to call my lawyer!" In my excitement, I fumbled with my cell phone.

When I got through to my attorney Scott and said, "They just got DPR!" A few moments of weighty silence followed before he responded. "You're shitting me." I heard shock in his voice.

Several thoughts tumbled over themselves in my head. *I don't have to play dead anymore. I no longer have to deal with this situation.* And then, over and over, *Oh my gosh, this is DPR! This is the real DPR!*

It felt weird, even surreal, to finally put a face to the mysterious persona I'd been communicating with and working for all this time. On seeing his picture plastered on the Internet, I couldn't help feeling startled even the second and third time that I saw it.

That kid is DPR? He's the one who wanted me dead?

To my surprise, I didn't hear from Carl until the next day. My excitement had cooled only a little by the time he called.

"You've probably heard about DPR," he said. I could hear the exhilaration in his voice. I could tell he was ecstatic. "You can go outside now, everything's okay, he's been arrested!"

"Yeah, I've heard," I said.

By then, however, I'd already moved on to a new phase. I'd begun to grow nervous for a different reason.

DPR's cronies and other people like him are going to think that I brought him down. If my name gets out, they're going to think I'm the rat. What's going to happen now?

The truth was, I still couldn't show my face. I had to stay in hiding.

Up until then I had been protected because nobody knew the true identity of Chronicpain and Flush. I had been safe, in the internet world at least, in a sort of anonymous cocoon. I'd heard that DPR have enforcers, killers in drug cartels and various gangs.

And now the police would be spilling their information about me.

Now I'm going to be exposed. There are still a lot of unknowns.

There was still a crooked cop out there who had framed me, set me up for a hit. I suspected that if the truth were known, he was the kind of man who would have killed me outright, just to get me out of the way, if he could have done it quietly.

The cloud that had lifted for a brief hour or two settled in once more.

I'm right back to where I was before. Oh, crap, what's going to happen now? How long am I going to go to prison for?

Within hour of the news of the arrest, I began getting death threats online—dozens of them, maybe as many as 200. One of the threats even promised to kill my wife, and described what the sender would do to my children and grandchildren, and went so far as to list the names and addresses of my grandkids.

Some of Ross's old "lieutenants" might well have been making those threats, drug dealers from the cartels and biker gangs.

Since I had a concealed-carry permit, I began packing a gun.

23: The Sinking of the Dread Pirate Roberts

Spanish Fork, Utah

Sometimes the legal system struggles to rehabilitate criminals. Sometimes it just tries to expunge them from the earth.

During the next few weeks, as I pondered my own legal fate, I kept my gun handy as I began to research my former employer and would-be murderer.

The "Dread Pirate Roberts"' real name is Ross William Ulbricht. He was born on March 27, 1984 into a well-to-do family and grew up in the Austin vicinity of Texas. He participated in Boy Scouts and even earned the rank of Eagle Scout. I learned that he attended West Ridge Middle School and Westlake High School in Austin, from which he graduated in 2002. It seemed like a fairly normal childhood to me.

After high school he headed for Dallas to attend the University of Texas on a full academic scholarship. That seemed impressive.

Ross graduated from UTD in 2006 with a bachelor's degree in physics, and went from there to Pennsylvania State University. There he entered a master's degree program in materials science and engineering and studied crystallography.

By the time Ross graduated from Penn State he'd lost interest in his major and become enamored of libertarian economic theory. He became fascinated with the political philosophy of Ludwig von Mises, supported Ron Paul for president, and participated in college debates to discuss his economic views.

He graduated from Penn State in 2009 and went home to Austin, where he found regular employment unsatisfying. He decided to become an entrepreneur.

However, his first attempts to start his own business failed. He eventually partnered with a friend to help build an online used bookstore, Good Wagon Books. His limited business success, and a rough breakup with his on-and-off girlfriend from Penn State, left him deeply dissatisfied with his life.

Even in 2009 Ross had contemplated the idea of building an online black market that would use Tor and bitcoin to evade law enforcement. By hosting his market as a Tor site, he knew he could hide its IP address, and so he experimented by selling his own home-grown magic mushrooms, a business that worked so well, he ran out of stock within hours.

Ross began to develop his online marketplace in 2010, as a side project to Good Wagon Books. He also kept a diary from time to time during the operating history of Silk Road. In his first entry he wrote about his situation prior to launching his site and predicted that he would make 2011 "a year of prosperity" through his new online venture. Ross may even have included a reference to Silk Road on his LinkedIn page, where he discussed his desire to "use economic theory as a means to abolish the use of coercion and aggression amongst mankind." He claimed, "I am creating an economic simulation to give people a first-hand experience of what it would be like to live in a world without the systemic use of force."

One author, Nathaniel Popper, thought the creation of Silk Road was an act of "sheer desperation" after Ross had exhausted, on his failed businesses, most of the nest egg he had out of college.

I don't know if I buy that. Ross seemed to me to be energetic, optimistic, and driven. Sure, as with any new entrepreneur, he was eager to succeed, but I suspect that he had a list of good qualities that would have served him well in just about any business. He was dedicated, frugal, hard-working, and knew how to network. His attributes were like a wish-list for applicants at schools like Harvard.

Having discovered Silk Road in its early phase, I clearly remembered when Ross had announced on the Silk Road site that his new name would be Dread Pirate Roberts, DPR.

The connection between Ross and "Dread Pirate Roberts" was made by Gary Alford, an IRS investigator working with the DEA on the Silk Road case, in mid-2013. When he was arrested, DPR was accused by the Federal Bureau of Investigation of being the "mastermind" behind Silk Road.

Several of the vendors and I had wondered sometimes where DPR was located, based on his communications patterns. After his arrest, I learned that he had moved to San Francisco sometime before then. He was taken into custody at the Glen Park branch of the San Francisco Public Library.

To prevent him from encrypting or deleting data on the laptop he was using to run the site, when he was arrested, a pair of agents staged a little act as quarreling lovers right behind him, and the man threatened to beat the woman. When Ross turned around from his table to see what was going on, a young female agent who had seated herself nearby, posing as a student, snatched his laptop computer and inserted a USB flash drive. It immediately cloned all the data on the laptop's hard drive. At that point, FBI Agent Chris Tarbell presented DPR with a warrant for his arrest. Since the laptop not only had him opened onto the Silk Road website and logged in as DPR, but also had his personal electronic journal and notes about how to run the site, the FBI caught him red-handed.

Ross Ulbricht was charged with money laundering, computer hacking, conspiracy to traffic narcotics, and procuring murder—my murder for starters, as well as some guys in Canada who had supposedly blackmailed him, along with others.

The charge of procuring murder was eventually dropped from the indictment. The FBI felt that they didn't need it. They had him on Kingpin charges that would send him to prison for life without the possibility of parole, but they wanted to keep the murder conspiracy charges in their "back pocket," just in case he was ever able to get out of prison on appeal. They had him solidly on those charges because of the photo Tonya and I had taken of my fake death, as well as the proof that he'd paid for a hit. This was all later factored into his sentence.

I learned that when DPR got proof of my murder, he fell silent for several minutes, then wrote that he "felt bad" about it, since he had never taken innocent blood before.

But he didn't feel badly enough to stop killing. The prosecutor was unable to prove that any of six other murders-for-hire that he contracted actually occurred, despite the fact that DPR paid $730,000 to have them carried out. From the evidence, it appears to me that at least one did occur. A man who tried to blackmail DPR was reportedly killed, though his body has ever been found. Let's just say that there are a lot of wooded spots in Canada that still ought to be searched.

The charge of procuring murder might eventually be dealt with in a separate trial pending in Maryland.

Not all of the information that came out made me feel comfortable. Ross had several "lieutenants" who worked with him, and I worried that some of them were searching for me.

About six weeks after Ross was arrested, someone logged into the Silk Road site using his name and password. That caused a lot of speculation. Some people online wondered if there might indeed be two DPRs. But others suspected that it was a cop, or perhaps someone pulling scams and trying to steal more money off of the site.

I believed the latter. The person who had framed me was still lurking about.

When Ross went on trial, his defense attorney asked if I would testify in his behalf, and I would have been happy to do so, but the judge intervened, knowing that my own case against the police might taint the case.

I considered flying to Maryland to watch the case as a spectator, but I had so many death threats being made against me, I didn't dare.

Instead, I got to read about how Ross was found guilty of money laundering, computer hacking, conspiracy to traffic fraudulent identity documents, and conspiracy to traffic narcotics by means of the internet, and was sentenced to life in prison without the possibility of parole. That caused me some real terror. The sentence seemed Draconian to me, considering that many heroin dealers in the US who are caught selling much larger amounts serve only ten years in prison.

At the same time, I had to remember that Ross had tried to kill me...

So I had drug dealers making threats, a crooked cop out to kill me, and my own trial date was still pending. It looked as if I didn't have a prayer.

24: Cops on the Run

Spanish Fork, Utah

I've never felt that I was a vindictive person, but when the cops started getting caught, man did the revenge taste sweet!

As Ross Ulbricht's case matured, I watched the prosecution closely, afraid that it might be a portent of what was in store for me.

Then one day in March, just a few weeks after DPR's sentencing, I got a call from my attorney.

He said, "Something big is going on. I don't know what it is exactly, but I think that Carl Force has been arrested."

My old friend Nob. I knew instantly that he had been arrested for corruption, and that he was the one who had stolen my money. His interest in bitcoin, his frequent phone calls. He was always trying to pull me in, befriend me in secret, while he played the tough cop in public.

A couple of days later I was invited to a meeting in Salt Lake. The meeting was to be held with agents from the FBI and AUSA attorneys from Oakland, California and Washington, D.C.

I still carried my gun on this trip, due to the death threats, and wondered what was in store.

I had met Tigran Gambaryan before, and he was always very cool and professional, but when I got to Salt Lake for our meeting, it was obvious that he was furious. Fortunately, he wasn't angry at me. He explained that they had come and were investigating crimes *against* me this time, as a victim. Indeed, he explained that the entire investigation was an effing nightmare, and he and Kathryn Haun explained what had happened. He used the f-word in every sentence, sometimes several times in the same sentence. I'll spare you all of the brooding imagery and just try to relate the tale.

Information about Carl's arrest hadn't been leaked to the public yet, but I was given an early peek into the case because this time, I was being investigated as a victim of a crime, not as a criminal. So, the tale began to unfold:

By October 2013, when DPR was arrested, Carl had spent two years working on the Baltimore-based task force investigating Silk Road. It turns out that during that time he'd also been cultivating some lucrative projects on the side. All of them were connected to bitcoin, which he seemed convinced would make him rich (and it would have).

He went through several schemes to extort money and pay bribes, but in October his plans began to fall apart. By then, government prosecutors had begun to sift through a mountain of evidence, but Carl had no idea how big it was.

He'd been treating DPR like his personal Bitcoin ATM for several months by that point, attempting to extort DPR one day and wrangling bitcoin bribes for fake information the next.

He'd even gone so far as to take money for the hit on me, without bothering to report it to his bosses. Well, he reported half of the money to his bosses, and then pocketed the other half.

Then, using another pseudonym, he sent a message to DPR warning that he knew that DPR had had me killed, and promising vengeance if DPR didn't pay a quarter of a million dollars. But DPR just ignored the threat.

Suddenly Carl no longer wanted to hold onto those bitcoins. He opened an account with Bitstamp, a bitcoin exchange in Slovenia that I'd told him about, where he thought he could turn bitcoins into cash quickly and quietly.

But when Carl opened Bitstamp account #557042 on October 12, 2013, it sealed his fate. He had tricked DPR into paying him more than 1,200 bitcoins, a cache worth more than a million dollars on today's market. Trying to launder those ill-gotten gains through Bitstamp was about the worst mistake Carl could've made, though he didn't know it at the time.

Oh, yeah, and we found that he'd stolen my bitcoins and my piddling little $3,000 Dwolla account, and another $350,000 from an investor on Silk Road.

Carl Force, it turned out, had many identities on Silk Road. He used an alias to pretend to be an FBI informant so that DPR would pay for information on impending busts under one guise, then he threatened to out DPR for killing me in another, hoping to extort a 250,000 dollar bribe.

Carl Force used a lot of encrypted communications, so that the feds never could tell exactly what kinds of crimes he might have committed. So there was a lot of confusion at the time.

As I learned how he had stolen money off Silk Road, it became clear that he'd stolen most of it from a single investor, not from the drug dealers who wanted me dead.

What? I wondered. That didn't make sense. I felt sure that he was the one who had betrayed me, who wanted me dead, but there was something "off" here. Was he the one who had set me up? Or had someone else robbed the drug dealers?

That is when they told me about his partner.

Investigating Carl ultimately led to Secret Service Agent Shaun Bridges, who worked on the same Baltimore task force with Carl and ran an even more profitable scheme. The AUSA in Oakland had gone looking for a rat in Baltimore and found two. Though they were friendly co-workers tasked to the same case, the government believes that each was apparently unaware of the other's scheme.

Here is how they were caught. When Carl decided to cash out his bitcoins, he opened his Bitstamp account as "Eladio Guzman Fuentes," an authorized undercover identity that he used as a DEA agent. With a Maryland driver's license, proof of residence, and Social Security card all connected to Mr. Fuentes, Carl believed he'd be in the clear, and would be able to convert his bitcoins into cash.

His documents ended up in the hands of Bitstamp's general counsel, George Frost, a journalist-turned-attorney who handled legal matters for the Bitcoin startup out of his quiet backyard office in Berkeley, California. When Mr. Frost looked at the identity documents sent by "Fuentes," they didn't check out.

"I can't tell you exactly how, but we knew they were sophisticated forgeries," Frost told an interviewer for Ars Technica, an online magazine.

Frost confronted Carl, who quickly confessed. He showed the Bitstamp lawyer his real ID, a Baltimore water bill, and his badge.

"I am a Special Agent with the Drug Enforcement Administration and learned about Bitcoin through my investigation of SILK ROAD," Carl wrote to Bitstamp, which provided his email to Ars. "I have attached a copy of my resumé and a scanned copy of my badge and credentials."

With that, Frost allowed Carl set up an account, but it still didn't sit right. Even if Carl was law enforcement, Frost wasn't sure he wanted him around. The new startup didn't need the headaches of being a launching platform for DEA undercover operations.

In the meantime, in November of 2014 Carl made a couple of large transactions, transferring first $34,000 and then $96,000 worth of bitcoins into a bank account.

Bitstamp allowed the withdrawals, but the lawyer in Frost continued to be suspicious. DEA credentials or not, he felt Carl's behavior was suspicious. So, Frost contacted FinCEN, a bureau of the Treasury Department that collects financial data to uncover possible crimes.

The contact person at FinCEN proved to be none other than Shaun Bridges, with whom Frost had worked before. The Secret Service has been part of the Department of Homeland Security since 2003, but it used to be under the Treasury.

"Bridges was a smart guy and seemed very conscientious," Frost recalled.

Shaun promised Frost he would refer the case to the Department of Justice's Public Integrity Section, the division that deals with public corruption, but nothing seemed to happen after that. The case just disappeared.

Meanwhile, Carl kept moving assets out of bitcoins. In December 2013 he paid off his mortgage in full. It had about $130,000 outstanding.

In April 2014, six months after DPR's arrest, Carl made another big withdrawal. This time he retrieved about $80,000.

Bitstamp employees went back and checked out Carl's IP addresses. They were all connected to Tor.

"Sometimes there's a good reason for using Tor, but it's a big red flag for us," said Frost.

In fact, maybe because of Carl, Bitstamp no longer allows accounts with Tor connections.

Carl explained that he used Tor for privacy, and "he didn't particularly want the NSA looking over his shoulder," Frost said. He thought the explanation seemed pretty fishy, but they allowed Carl to make the withdrawal.

On April 28, 2014, Carl tried a fourth withdrawal. That one was his biggest yet, as he tried to move more than $200,000 in bitcoins. This time Frost decided to freeze the account until he could get more specific answers. He'd still had no response from the federal authorities to whom he'd reported Carl's curious behavior.

On May 1, Mr. Frost tried an alternate tactic. He had a scheduled meeting with someone whose eyes wouldn't roll back at the mere mention of bitcoins. Kathryn Haun, an assistant United States attorney (AUSA) in San Francisco, was the DOJ's first digital currency coordinator. Also at the meeting was Tigran Gambaryan, a 28-year-old special agent with the Internal Revenue Service in nearby Oakland.

After the meeting, Frost was blunt about his suspicions of Carl. "I'm an old reporter and I really smell a rat here," he told them.

Haun asked him what was up.

"For one thing, he's using his undercover name and undercover credentials," Frost explained.

That *was* a bit weird, Ms. Haun thought. But at first, she considered it most likely a sign of sloppy undercover work rather than criminality. Besides, assigning agents to investigate other agents wasn't a decision to be made lightly. Ms. Haun thought the case seemed thin. Still, she urged Frost to send on what he had.

Gambaryan was interested, too. The Oakland-based agent was deeply intrigued by technology in general and bitcoins in particular. He'd relished the stories of his colleagues who had worked on the Silk Road case, including fellow IRS special agent Gary Alford, who had been the first to identify DPR through a little Google-fu of his own.

Gambaryan also knew about the tensions between the Silk Road investigative teams in Baltimore and New York, but Frost's sudden aside after the meeting raised the prospect that something more sinister than just agency rivalry was going on. It was a distant possibility, but why, Gambaryan thought, would anyone involved in the Silk Road case try to cash out large quantities of bitcoins?

Ms. Haun and Mr. Gambaryan were on the fence about the value of investigating it at all. But the very next day Carl did something that made an investigation all but inevitable.

"Could you please delete my transaction history to date?" Carl asked Bitstamp's customer service in an email. "It is cumbersome to go through records back to November 2013 for my accountant."

The request put Frost on high alert. He already suspected this DEA agent had gone rogue, and now it appeared that he was trying to destroy evidence. He called Bitstamp's Slovenian service team and told them not to delete anything. Then Frost called Ms. Haun. She opened an investigation the same day, still not sure if it would amount to much.

With a formal investigation now underway, Gambaryan finally found a case that seemed tailor-made to his interests. From the second he'd started working at the IRS Oakland office in 2011, he had informally chatted with various bitcoin startups, as eager to learn more about their industry as I had been. That was how I'd discovered Silk Road.

Gambaryan had studied accounting in college and had taken his first job at the California Franchise Tax Board. Soon after, he decided to move up the law enforcement ladder, and the Internal Revenue Service beckoned.

While Gambaryan was deeply interested in the topic, he'd never actually worked a bitcoin case before. To investigate Carl, he had to trace the digital currency in the same way he'd learned to hunt down black-market money enumerated in "regular" currency.

"I started looking at it, and I was like, 'I have no idea what I'm looking at, it's just a bunch of numbers,'" he said.

He was starting at ground zero, but he also knew it was possible. Bitcoin's greatest feature was also its greatest liability for would-be criminals. Everything was on the record, forever. The blockchain is basically a giant public ledger.

If Gambaryan could pull Carl's financial records, find his bitcoin activity, and then match that with transaction records already locked away in the government's Silk Road database, he would know whether he really had a case. So, in an unassuming cubicle in an upper floor of the twin towers federal building in downtown Oakland, Gambaryan began that painstaking process, learning how to follow particular threads of bitcoins moving in and out of Silk Road.

Ms. Haun began to work the case as well, situated in the federal high-rise a few blocks from San Francisco's City Hall. She had an obvious place to start: Shaun Bridges, the Secret Service agent who Frost still believed was his friend in the government.

On May 6, the investigating duo got Bridges on the phone. Ms. Haun introduced herself and explained the allegations against Carl. She expected Bridges to react with, at a minimum, serious concern. Instead, presenting himself to Frost and the others as the government's point man for all things bitcoin, he questioned her authority.

"What is a federal prosecutor in San Francisco doing, investigating anything going on in Baltimore?" he asked, as Ms. Haun later recalled in interviews. "Why do you have any jurisdiction here?"

That set off more alarm bells. Ms. Haun and Gambaryan had questions about government agents possibly mishandling funds, and now Bridges was getting defensive. Ms. Haun remembered saying, "What is a Secret Service agent in Baltimore doing, going all over the world telling people you're the exclusive point of contact for the U.S. government?"

After they hung up, Haun and Gambaryan agreed that Bridges seemed sketchy. For the time being, though, they had to move ahead with Carl's case without any help from Bridges, the man who allegedly could have told them the most about it.

As the days turned into weeks, Gambaryan got hold of the Silk Road database and immersed himself in the details of DPR's case, taking note of every interaction that Carl had with DPR. He reviewed Carl's videotaped undercover interactions and case reports. He hunted through every message that Carl, in his various online personas, had exchanged with DPR. He had to know what Carl had done on Silk Road to find out whether he'd taken money from the site.

Carl's "official" undercover account, the only one Gambaryan knew about initially was, you guessed it, Nob. Using that account, Carl had gotten DPR's attention. The method he'd used wasn't subtle. He'd sent a message reading "Nob business proposal," stating that he wanted to straight-up purchase the whole Silk Road site. DPR had suggested a price of $1 billion, far more than what Nob had in mind. But the somewhat off-the-wall conversation served its purpose. As Nob, Carl had forged a relationship with DPR.

After a few months of working undercover, on December 7, 2012 Force proposed a deal. He complained to DPR that

Silk Road sellers only want "very small amounts of drugs" and that "it isn't really worth it for me to do below ten kilos." DPR then told Nob he would try to locate a buyer for such a large quantity. The next day DPR wrote back, "I think we have a buyer for you. One of my staff is sending the details."

That unfortunate buyer was none other than me. Or, at least, DPR wanted to sell the idea that I was a buyer so that he could move the large amounts of merchandise that Carl said he wanted to move. So, Carl apparently pushed the idea of sending me some cocaine so that he could arrest me as soon as I opened my mail.

Oddly, given their methods of investigating me, that part of the investigation was considered legal. It turned out that my willingness to cooperate and accept the proffer agreement, including giving them my account password of Flush, led directly to the downfall not just of the Dread Pirate Roberts, but also Carl Force and Shaun Bridges.

The very night that they got my password, someone logged in as me and started taking huge amounts of bitcoins out of an account called Number13. That was the investor account that Carl Force robbed.

Other sellers had bitcoins disappear from their accounts, too. By the time DPR and Inigo figured out what was going on, roughly 20,000 bitcoins, worth about $350,000 at that time (or $16 million at today's prices), had disappeared.

Yes, the missing $350,000 for which I was nearly drowned in that Marriott bathtub. The money that my court-appointed attorney kept begging me to confess to stealing. The money that Justin Herring kept trying to get me to confess to stealing, going so far as to tell me that I'd even be able to keep it if I confessed. It was the same money that Shaun Bridges and Carl Force kept demanding that I confess to stealing.

Apparently, DPR had gone ballistic, and figured that I was behind it. After a little thinking about who might help him teach me a lesson, DPR naturally turned to the man who had just introduced himself as an experienced criminal: Nob.

Carl, good old Nob, had been all too happy to help, much to my distress. When DPR had changed his mind and asked, "Can you change the order to *execute rather than torture?*" Carl/Nob had said he'd do the job for $80,000 in bitcoins, half payable up front, and DPR agreed. That's what led to the NCIS-style photography session in our bathroom.

I learned later that when DPR got the pictures of my fake dead body, he said that he was "a little disturbed, but I'm ok. . . . I'm new to this kind of thing." DPR had added that "I don't think I've done the wrong thing," and "I'm sure I will call on you again at some point, though I hope I won't have to."

Carl told DPR that I'd died of heart failure after being tortured, and on February 28, 2014, reported that my body had been "completely destroyed." Carl asked for the final $40,000 and DPR sent it promptly. Carl pocketed that money and never reported it to his bosses.

But Carl wasn't the one who'd actually stolen all of the $350,000 in the first place.

As I said before, half of Carl's "hit" money was handed over to the government. But he'd developed a few more ideas about how to get paid, ideas he wasn't quite so forthcoming about.

On April 1, 2013, DPR received this cryptic message from a new account called Death From Above: "I know that you had something to do with Curtis Green's disappearance and death. Just wanted to let you know that I'm coming for you. Tuque. You are a dead man. Don't think you can elude me. De Oppresso Liber."

After a short back-and-forth, Death From Above tried to extort $250,000 from DPR.

The messages were from Carl. Gambaryan discovered it only because Carl got sloppy. In one of his official reports, he left video footage of himself typing to DPR as DFA, Death From Above.

The extortion attempt didn't work. It took five days for DPR to reply: "Your threats and all of the other aren't going to deter me... Stop messaging me and go find something else to do."

Having failed at that gambit, Carl decided to use a carrot rather than a stick. Under the Nob personality, Force convinced DPR that he had access to a corrupt Department of Justice employee who went by the name of Kevin. That month, DPR paid Nob 400 bitcoins, then worth about $40,000, for Kevin's "counter-intelligence" information. Two months later, DPR paid an additional 525 bitcoins.

In Carl's regular reports to his superiors, known as a DEA "6," he described the first payment. But in regard to the second, Force wrote, "DPR made no such payment."

As far as what information Carl sold to DPR, that's unclear. It had to be worthwhile, something that DPR would see as valuable, and it appears that Carl was giving information on the FBI's investigation of Silk Road, warning DPR of impending raids.

All of Carl's efforts seemed to me, at least, to be designed to increase DPR's fear, to make him feel that his freedom and his very life were in jeopardy, so that he could be more easily extorted.

Amongst DPR's and Nob's July 31, 2013 to August 4, 2013 encrypted messages, which were preserved in the seized Silk Road server, there was only one left in cleartext. DPR noted that he had paid the 525 bitcoins "as requested." Carl, corresponding as Nob, wrote back just two words. "Use PGP!" In short, Carl was asking DPR to use only encrypted text when discussing money.

That was enough. Gambaryan could see that a single payment of 525 bitcoins had gone to another one of Force's Bitcoin wallets. It happened exactly when DPR said that he'd paid.

"Ross' screwup was what got Carl caught," Gambaryan told Ars.

But Carl had yet another scheme. He created a third Silk Road identity called French Maid and offered to sell DPR information about the government's investigation into the site for another $100,000 in bitcoins. Again, DPR paid. Again, the money went into one of Carl's personal accounts.

It isn't clear what, if anything, Carl told DPR after getting that cash. A daily log file from Ulbricht's computer

337

mentions French Maid. The document notes that DPR paid $100,000 but didn't hear back.

On May 30, 2014, Ms. Haun led a proffer session for Carl, with Gambaryan at her side. The concept of a proffer, what I'd been offered myself, is that it allows a defendant to come clean and give up useful information in exchange for a shorter sentence. The session was conducted as a video conference with Ms. Haun and Gambaryan in San Francisco, and Force and his lawyer, Ivan Bates, across the country in Baltimore.

Carl admitted working as Nob and improperly taking bitcoins that belonged to the government. However, he tried to play it off as a big misunderstanding. He didn't know where or how to transmit them to the government because Bitcoin was a new technology the government wasn't equipped for. To boot, Carl argued that he'd profited on the government's behalf as the price of Bitcoin went up.

That, obviously, didn't hold water. A newbie agent might have some confusion about the right way to hold evidence, but it didn't come close to excusing Force's behavior.

In an interview, Ms. Haun posited a hypothetical. "If the courtroom is closed at the end of the day, and there's $20,000 cash in evidence, I might not know where to put it," she said. "But I know not to put it in my bank account."

At that point, Ms. Haun knew Carl had acted illegally, but she still didn't know how far he'd gone. He was asked directly, "Have you heard of an account called 'French Maid?' Have you heard of 'Death from Above?'"

Carl denied knowing anything about those accounts.

After the proffer session, opinion was split among the agents and lawyers in San Francisco as to whether Carl was telling the truth. For her part, Ms. Haun felt quite sure he was lying.

Gambaryan went back to the vast Silk Road database. It took some time, but he was able to confirm Ms. Haun's suspicions that Carl was indeed both French Maid and Death from Above. Carl had left the particular version of PGP in his e-mail signatures in his various personae.

Carl was finally boxed in. The fact that he'd lied during the proffer session, as I had feared so much doing myself, meant that everything he had said could be used against him.

For his part, Shaun Bridges had continued to engage in odd behavior since that first phone call early in the investigation of Carl. In mid-June 2014, Ms. Haun and Gambaryan attended a Europol meeting in the Netherlands. Before returning to California, they decided to fly on to Slovenia and meet with Bitstamp executives in person to discuss Carl's case.

By early December 2014, Ms. Haun was just about ready to charge Carl. But then Gambaryan made a startling discovery. He was able to determine that the 525 bitcoin payment had come directly from DPR himself, by manually cross-referencing Carl's and DPR's bitcoin transactions. He confirmed this with the help of a new website called Wallet Explorer.

This new site, like no other before it, could accurately trace the history of bitcoin payments and wallets. Moreover, its capabilities included mapping wallets into known "clusters," which means mapping addresses to known entities like Silk Road, Coinbase, and other large Bitcoin players.

But there was more to this discovery than just DPR's transactions with Carl. After becoming more comfortable with his blockchain analysis, Gambaryan strongly suspected there was another bad actor. The dozens of hours he'd spent tracing the movements of bitcoins through the blockchain showed some currency being moved in small groups, while others were bouncing around as large chunks. There were two different styles of criminals. Carl had made some simplistic transfers of money using his own name. But Gambaryan saw another, more complicated, set of transfers as well.

On Christmas Eve 2014, Gambaryan called Ms. Haun at 11:00 PM to tell her that there was new, strong evidence to suggest that the Silk Road bitcoin heist was specifically linked to the Baltimore Silk Road Task Force. The IRS special agent had always thought that Baltimore was connected somehow, because they were the only ones who had access to me, but he couldn't prove it.

"It didn't make sense for Green to do it," Gambaryan pointed out. "He was in their custody and cooperating."

But as Gambaryan explained to Ms. Haun, one of his colleagues, IRS special agent Gary Alford, had found older correspondence between his two targets, Carl and Shaun. On January 23, 2013, Carl had e-mailed Bridges, asking him to replenish a DEA-controlled Silk Road account called TrustUsJones. Bridges did so from another Silk Road account, Number13.

It wasn't clear with bulletproof certainty that Bridges and Number13 were one and the same, but it certainly suggested, at the very least, that the Baltimore Task Force had access to some Silk Road-based bitcoin accounts. Investigators now had a clear direction to go in.

As they considered the charges against Carl, Gambaryan and Ms. Haun worked under the theory that he had also been responsible for the massive theft from Silk Road drug dealers. After all, he was a known corrupt cop who had been in the room when I produced the "keys to the kingdom."

But they thought it was worth double-checking, even if it was a slow and cumbersome process. Armed with Gambaryan's new revelation, they determined that the Number13 account had sent the stolen bitcoins to Mt. Gox, a Japan-based bitcoin exchange that had since been raided by investigators and gone bankrupt. Gambaryan had to use a mutual legal assistance treaty (MLAT) procedure to get financial records from the Japanese bankruptcy trustee.

Those records showed that the Mt. Gox money had cashed out to a Fidelity account registered to Quantum Investments, a company that Bridges had amazingly registered in his own name, using his actual home address in a Maryland city somewhere between Baltimore and Washington, DC.

What's more, just two days before the raid, the owner had pulled all of his money out.

From there, the next part was easy. A subpoena to Fidelity took less than a day to come back, showing who had created the Quantum account. It was Shaun Bridges.

The Secret Service was notified that Bridges was under investigation and suspected of wrongdoing. The usual process would have been for Bridges to be put on some kind of leave. Instead, on March 15, 2015, he resigned. To Kathryn Haun and Gambaryan, that strongly suggested they had hit the target. Bridges was a second, bigger thief, and he thought himself the smarter one.

Ms. Haun brought in her boss, Assistant United States Attorney William Frentzen. He had supervised her on the Ripple Labs case, a related cryptocurrency. A 20-year veteran of the Department of Justice, Frentzen had also worked with her on organized crime cases.

"The hair stood up on the back of my neck," he recalled in his interview with Ars. "There's two of them."

Bridges was also offered a proffer session, and his lawyer said he wanted to cooperate. They flew out together to San Francisco to meet with Ms. Haun and her team in person. But Bridges was neither conciliatory nor apologetic. Instead, he was arrogant and unrepentant.

"The missing link, you don't have," Bridges told Ms. Haun from across the conference table.

He thought that the Mt. Gox records, which showed the stolen bitcoins moving from Silk Road into his Quantum account, would be impossible to get. Bridges had even tried to make them impossible to get.

When his Baltimore team instituted a civil seizure proceeding against Mt. Gox, Bridges had tried to go to Japan to collect the records himself.

"We would charge you and try you without those," Ms. Haun told him plainly.

But there was more bad news for Shaun Bridges. She and Gambaryan already did have the exact records he thought would be missing forever.

Usually, the dynamic in a proffer session is frank.

"We've got you, don't bullshit us," Ms. Haun said. "Yet he was untruthful. He thought he was the smartest guy in the room and no one else in the government would be able to 'get it,' to understand what he did."

Charges were filed against both Carl Force and Shaun Bridges, with Gambaryan's name at the bottom, on March 30, 2015.

Within a month, Bridges pleaded guilty. Weeks later, on July 1, 2015, Carl did, too.

Carl went peacefully to prison. When he was sentenced, I wasn't allowed to testify at his hearing, but I later learned that he pleaded for leniency due to problems with mental illness. It turned out that this had been his first undercover case since he was institutionalized for mental illness a couple of years earlier. The judge didn't buy his excuses, but he sounded to me like a broken man.

Bridges was ultimately sentenced to 71 months, while Carl was given 78 months.

Unlike Carl, Shaun Bridges didn't go as quietly. He brought his boss in to plead for leniency based upon his exemplary past service. He had been assigned to protect the first family, after all, and as a marksman scored a perfect 300 out of 300 on his field tests.

He claimed that he had made a simple error of judgment, but the judge disagreed, since he showed a clear pattern of corruption.

I did get to go to Baltimore to his sentencing hearing and tell my side of the story, confront the man who did his best to frame me and get me killed. It felt great!

During their respective sentencing hearings, Carl Force did not speak, but Bridges did.

"I knew when I turned in Carl Force that it would ultimately lead to me," Bridges told the court. "I mean, the person turning him in worked with him; they're obviously going to look at me. But I accept that. I don't diminish one bit of it here."

Bridges also said he wanted to "apologize to everybody" and acknowledged that he "accepts full responsibility" for his actions.

However, while the judge and everyone else, including Ars, believed that Bridges' story was effectively over, he was likely the only one in the room who knew that it wasn't.

Two days before Bridges was set to report to prison, he asked the judge for permission to turn himself in a day early due to snowy weather conditions that could possibly impede the 10-hour drive from Baltimore to his assigned prison in New Hampshire. US District Judge Richard Seaborg granted this request.

Within hours, investigators suspected that Bridges wasn't going to make the drive after all. Instead, they anticipated that he would try to flee the country. When interviewed, Gambaryan declined to explain exactly how the authorities figured that out.

Bridges was taken into custody for the second time on January 28, 2016, arrested at his home. Tigran Gambaryan and a team of about 20 agents surrounded the house in an affluent neighborhood outside Baltimore. The agents drew guns, and they ordered Bridges to open the door or they would break it down. Bridges opened the door.

In two bags, the former Secret Service agent was carrying falsified ID documents, a notarized copy of his passport, a passport card, and corporate records for three offshore companies, located in Nevis, Belize, and Mauritius. One of them had been created on October 28, 2015, well after he'd pled guilty. He also had a laptop that he was forbidden to use by court order and he had two bulletproof vests that he'd stolen from the Secret Service.

It was later discovered that he had tainted perhaps dozens of investigations into criminal activity dealing with cryptocurrency, for his own gain.

So, Shaun Bridges was rearrested while trying to escape, and the judge added another two years to his sentence.

Despite his guilty plea, Bridges has also filed an appeal of his case. It's an unusual move, since Bridges, like most defendants who take a deal with prosecutors, waived his rights to an appeal.

Meanwhile, court documents unsealed in early July 2016 show that prosecutors suspect Bridges of additional thefts, including $700,000 that was seized from various Bitstamp accounts on Bridges' orders.

His lawyer, Davina Pujari, filed an unusual brief on August 8, 2016, saying that the arguments Bridges wanted her to make were "legally frivolous." She also asked the judge to allow her to be removed as Bridges' lawyer.

Despite the mountain of evidence uncovered by Ms. Haun, Gambaryan, and several others, two underlying questions remain unanswered. How much did Carl and Bridges collaborate? And was anyone else in the Baltimore Task Force corrupt, too?

The answer to the first remains unclear. Richard Evans, an assistant United States attorney in the DOJ's Public Integrity Section, and one of the prosecutors present for Bridges' December 2015 sentencing, said as much to the judge.

"We've not revealed any evidence that would indicate that [Force and Bridges were collaborating]," he said. "In a small task force, when you've got corrupt agents, one would think they would possibly talk about that. But we've not recovered any evidence to suggest that. And all we've got is that they were operating in separate silos, doing it on their own."

It still isn't completely clear whether Bridges and Carl collaborated, if at all. They were at least friendly, and each had an "offline" interest in Bitcoin. They texted each other about price increases and boasted about the money they were making.

"There's nothing that I found that suggests they were working together, which is crazy," Gambaryan said.

This lingering mystery may never be solved for certain. But one condition of both of men's sentences is that they are forbidden from communicating with each other.

Personally, I suspect that they were in collusion. I keep remembering how Carl Force, as soon as I revealed how to login to Silk Road, asked Shaun Bridges if there was somewhere else he had to be, sending him away, so that I was framed for theft within hours. And I can't help recalling how many times Carl told me not to talk to anyone about the case but him and Shaun Bridges.

"The whole case made me sick from start to finish," Frentzen said. "These are people that we work with every day."

As to whether others on the Baltimore Task Force were involved in corrupt activities, it's also hard to know for sure. But after months of investigation, no one else has been charged.

Homeland Security Investigations Special Agent Jared Der-Yeghiayan testified at trial that there was at least one other federal agent operating on the Silk Road, under the handle Mr. Wonderful. DPR's own files show that another user named "alpacino," whom he believed to be from the DEA, was leaking info to him. This could have been Carl, or it might have been another agent.

George Frost, the Bitstamp lawyer who kicked off the whole saga, remains convinced there are more suspects at large.

"It looks like there are still people out there that are involved," he said.

And new research into Shaun Bridges indicates that he may have put his sticky fingers into several more as-yet undiscovered pies.

25: Getting My Day in Court

January, 2016

Baltimore, Maryland

When a person is accused of a grievous crime, the person's life is often destroyed in the media circus that follows. The accuser usually just goes free.

I finally got to fly to Baltimore for my day in court to answer the charges against me. I felt anxious, nervous, knowing that I would go to prison just like everyone else involved with this case. Yet I was fully prepared to "do my time."

My attorney explained that there wasn't any sense in pleading not guilty to the drug charges. Even though the case against me, made by the DEA and Secret Service, had been falsified and corrupted due to the actions of certain officers, if that case was thrown out, the FBI would simply refile the charges.

So, I went before the court to plead guilty to dealing drugs, even though I wasn't, and I planned to beg for leniency, just like all of the other defendants.

I made the following statement:

"I was an employee of Silk Road from approximately November 2012 until January 2013. I got involved in SR because I was interested in Bitcoin and SR was the biggest marketplace for Bitcoin. I also had an interest in harm reduction related to drug use. Initially I just chatted on the forum, and that led to DPR hiring me to work for SR. I was basically employed as a customer service rep, assisting people to use the site. I never used illegal drugs and I never intended to be directly involved in illegal drug deals.

"In January 2013 federal agents stormed into my home and arrested me on drug charges. According to federal agents, DPR paid an undercover agent to murder me. The agents took photos as they faked my murder. I did not know the identity of DPR or any other user of SR. I never stole from DPR, SR or any SR users. On the advice of my attorney, I cannot give any further details, as I still face serious federal charges."

The judge found me guilty, but I was left hanging for many months as I waited for sentencing.

The sentencing phase of my trial didn't come until January of 2016—more than two years after I'd pled guilty.

I was fully prepared to get forty years in prison but hoped that it might be reduced to four years. But either way, I knew that jail time was what I deserved.

I reasoned that it was only four weeks after the holidays. I hoped that the judge might be in a lenient mood.

As I entered the court building, I saw dozens of old faces—AUSAs, agents from the FBI, DEA, Secret Service, and Homeland Security. I figured that they had all lined up to testify against me. There looked to be about twenty of them.

The judge who reviewed my case appeared stern, and to tell the truth, when I sat quivering in my chair in fear, and was asked to rise, I was shaking badly. It was almost like an out-of-body experience, where I felt as if I were watching myself from a distance.

But that's when I got the surprise of my life. As we moved to sentencing, the prosecution itself began to beg for leniency. AUSA Kathryn Haun told the story of how I had been arrested, setup by corrupt cops, and had to fake my own death in order to evade my killers. She told how I had cooperated with the police from the very beginning and had suffered ever since, being literally imprisoned in my own home as I feared for my life.

The cops in the room all watched, and I expected that at any moment one of them might object and begin to bad-mouth me, but no one ever did.

When the judge agreed that this was one of the most egregious miscarriages of justice that he'd ever seen, he handed down a sentence of "time served."

It took me a few moments to figure out what that meant. I was in shock. It meant that I was sentenced to just two days in jail, the time I'd spent in the jail in Spanish Fork.

Oh, there was another four years of supervision, but that doesn't amount to much—just a phone call to my probation officer, not the frequent drug tests that I had been having to take while I awaited sentencing.

I broke down and wept in relief as he handed my life back to me. Afterward, the cops all smiled in joy, and many of them rushed forward to pat me on the back and apologize. "I'm sorry that I ever misbelieved you," one said. "I really did think that you had stolen that money!" "Will you forgive me," another said as he hugged me. "I was just trying to do my job."

I think I practically danced out of the courtroom, and I couldn't wait to call Tonya and tell her the good news.

As I learned afterward, my sentencing happened within a couple of days of Shaun Bridges being rearrested for trying to flee the country.

We all went to jail—me, the Dread Pirate Roberts, and the cops who arrested us. I still don't know what to think of it all.

I was guilty of working on the Silk Road site. Though I didn't buy or sell drugs myself, one could say that I was enabling others who did. Mea Culpa.

If I had considered this more deeply, maybe I would never have gotten involved. There have sure been plenty of times when I have wished that I had walked away.

Instead I had listened to Ross Ulbricht and his libertarian views, and I dared to wonder if he was right. Ross believed that the criminal activity associated with dealing drugs was probably more dangerous than the drugs themselves. By legalizing drugs, he believed, we could get rid of the policing policies, reduce overcrowding in the prisons, and so on.

While Silk Road was in business, it attracted over a million clients. In that year, the number of gun deaths in the US dropped dramatically, almost 20 percent, since the users didn't have to interact with anyone more dangerous than their mailman.

But at the same time, the number of overdose deaths by opioid addicts rose, so that the numbers evened out.

So DPR was partly right. The people who died were the ones who took the drugs, victims of their own addiction.

Now, after considering his libertarian views, I'm not convinced. I love freedom, and we all want to be free. But let's face it, addicts aren't really free, are they? They can't make well-considered decisions, and many are incapable of considering the consequences of their addiction for their children, their parents, and loved ones.

So Ross is also partly wrong.

I see the addicts as victims. Twenty percent of all people who take opioids for pain become addicted. Seventeen percent of people who use cannabis become addicted, while about seven percent of alcohol users do. These are the people I was trying to save, those people who are victims of their own biology. I don't want them to die or just be thrown away by society.

Silk Road got shut down, and perhaps that is a good thing. The world is a safer place. But then it was reopened three months later, by one of DPR's captains, and Silk Road 2.0 got shut down.

People learned from Ross's mistakes. He was a single, driven kid with a laptop and an idea. He didn't know how to program, and perhaps that more than anything led to his capture.

But other people have created teams of savvy programmers, started new businesses like Silk Road, and right now there are a dozen other sites out there that do far more business than Silk Road ever did.

So maybe the world is a more dangerous place.

I think that our laws exist in order to try to bring peace and prosperity to people, in most cases. We make it illegal for minors to drink because we know that many of them are incapable of making a wise decision in the matter. That makes sense. The government demands that we be responsible for our actions.

We rely upon our government to create roads and build public utilities and police our country, and I suspect that if I was libertarian enough, I'd say we don't need that.

But the truth is that we do need it. We do need to care for each other, to take responsibility.

Here is what pisses me off, though: as citizens, our government demands that we act responsibly, but in far too many cases, I don't see them doing the same.

I see Democrats and Republicans who are so polarized that they aren't able to "walk across the aisle" and try to take action to fix our problems with things like health care, the budget deficit, or white-collar crime. Instead, they practice obstructionism to the point that some of them ought to be tried for treason.

I see a legal system that is shabby and often corrupt. If you want to know what I mean, just do a Google search to find out how many DEA agents have been arrested for murder in the past couple of years.

I see a crumbling infrastructure in America, where our roads and bridges have long been third-rate when compared to the infrastructures in Europe.

I see politicians making grandiose promises during political campaigns, only to renege on them within minutes of being elected.

I see families being ripped apart at the border by Republicans, while Democrats foolishly do their best to create sanctuary cities in order to give safe haven to foreign criminals.

I could go on for hours, hell, I want to go on for hours, but what I am seeing everywhere is Fake Government—corruption, avoidance of responsibility, laziness, stupidity, and avarice.

Trump says that he wants to "drain the swamp," but when you do that, the snakes and alligators all just crawl off into hiding.

So my opinions have changed radically in the past few years. I think that it is time for a revolution in America, a moral revolution, where each of us step up and work to put things right.

We can begin by voting, by stepping up to the plate and taking positions of leadership in our local communities, but perhaps we need to do far more than that.

I think that we need to clean up the waste and corruption that we see in our government.

It's our government. We pay for it, and if we don't demand the services we've paid for, then all of us, including our children and grandchildren, will continue to suffer.

I was asked to testify at Shaun Bridges sentencing, and so I made one last trip to Baltimore, and I did my best to get the judge to lock him up. He had betrayed the trust of his company, and though DPR got sent to prison for life for, in part, trying to have me executed, Shaun is the one who set me up, robbed the drug dealers, and tried to frame me for the crime so that I'd be killed.

He got sentenced to just under six years for his "betrayal" of the public trust, as the judge put it.

While I was there for the sentencing of Agent Shaun Bridges, I got to speak to Ross's mother, Lyn Ulbricht, a blonde and petite woman with a charming personality and an obvious love for her son. She has started a campaign to get her son freed, convinced that her son was illegally imprisoned, but unfortunately the Supreme Court has recently rejected her appeal for justice.

She likes to site the kangaroo nature of the court, where evidence of corruption was ignored. She alleges that Chuck Schumer called for the destruction of Silk Road himself, that the task force to dismantle it was set up in his jurisdiction within hours, that all of those arrested were carted off to be put on trial in Baltimore, regardless of where they lived, that the judge was hand-picked and appointed by Schumer, that the judge was overly harsh on sentencing, and so on. She asks, "Isn't there supposed to be a separation between the executive branch of the government and the legal branch, just to ensure that we don't get such kinds of abuse?"

She's right.

Yet it happens. If you anger the wrong politician, you'll find that your taxes suddenly get audited or the building permit on your home won't go through—or you'll get a bunch of government cocaine sent to your house so that you find yourself arrested for opening your mail.

I like Lyn, I decided, much as I liked her son. She seems like a good person.

We had breakfast together, and afterward she asked if I would help carry her bags down to the taxi. I didn't tell her about my bad back. I just lugged the packages down, and we chatted away, me and the mom of my attempted murderer, walking off into the bright sunlight of a Baltimore morning, and neither one of us were good guys or bad guys, as if we could wear labels.

We were all just people.

Printed in Great Britain
by Amazon